PENGUIN BOOKS

The Chibok Girls

Helon Habila is an Associate Professor of Creative Writing at George Mason University, USA. He was born in Nigeria and worked as a journalist in Lagos. His novels include *Waiting for an Angel, Measuring Time* and *Oil on Water,* and he is the editor of *The Granta Book of the African Short Story.* He has won many awards, including the Commonwealth Prize for Best First Novel, the Caine Prize and, most recently, the Windham-Campbell Prize. Helon Habila has been a contributing editor of the *Virginia Quarterly Review* since 2004, and he is a regular reviewer for the *Guardian.* He lives in Virginia, USA, with his wife and three children.

D1440208

The Chibok Girls
The Boko Haram Kidnappings and Islamist Militancy in Nigeria

Helon Habila

PENGUIN BOOKS

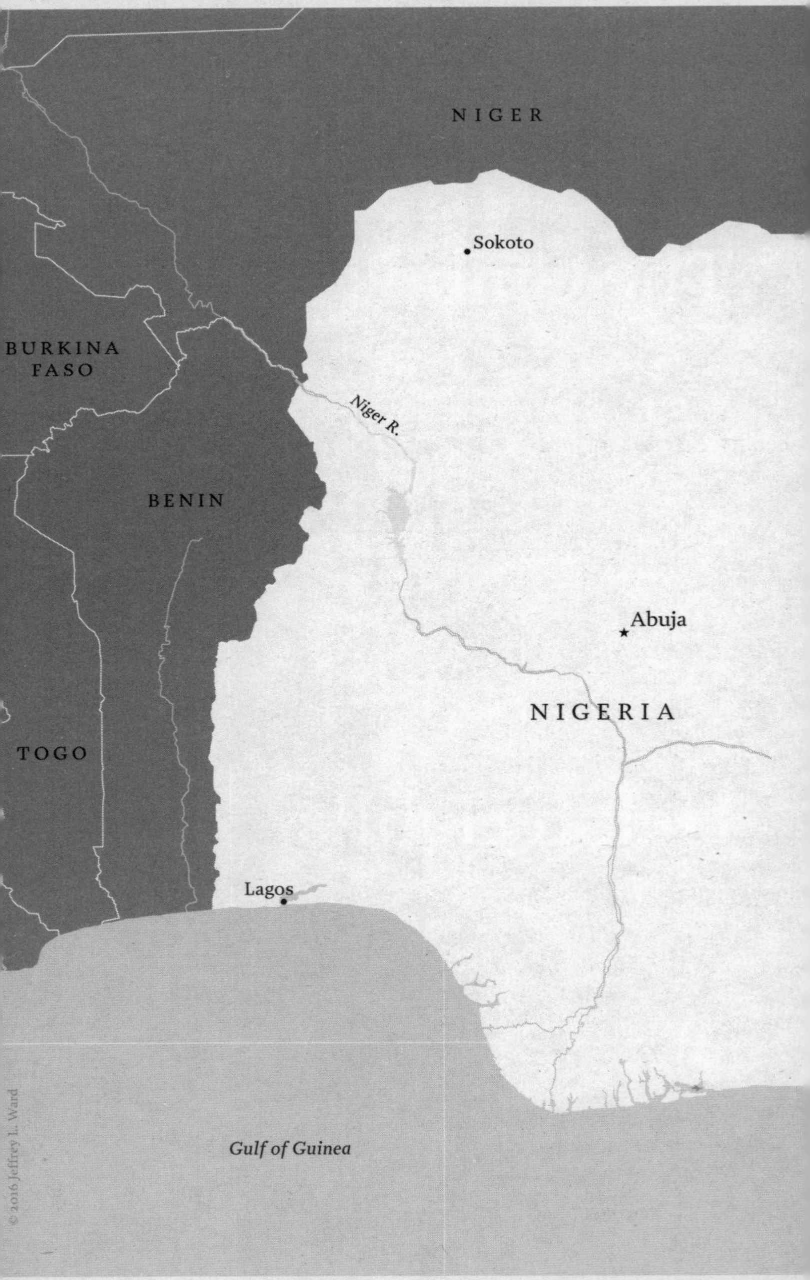
NIGER
Sokoto
BURKINA FASO
Niger R.
BENIN
Abuja
NIGERIA
TOGO
Lagos
Gulf of Guinea

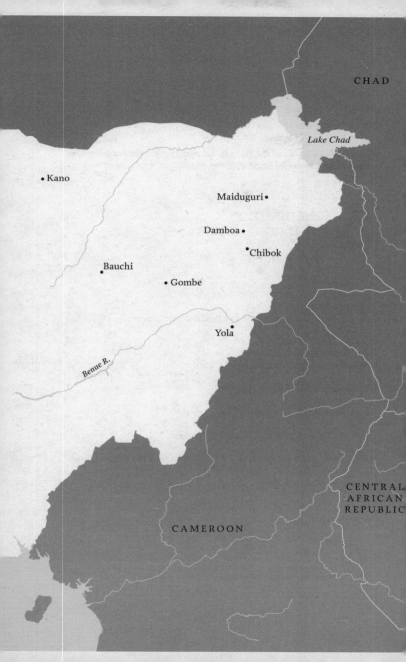

PENGUIN BOOKS

UK | USA | Canada | Ireland | Australia
India | New Zealand | South Africa

Penguin Books is part of the Penguin Random House group of companies
whose addresses can be found at global.penguinrandomhouse.com.

Penguin
Random House
UK

First published in the United States of America by
Columbia Global Reports 2016
First published in Great Britain as a Penguin Special 2017
001

Copyright © Helon Habila, 2016
Afterword copyright © Helon Habila, 2017

Map design by Jeffrey L. Ward

Printed in Great Britain by Clays Ltd, St Ives plc

A CIP catalogue record for this book is available from the British Library

ISBN: 978−0−241−98089−7

www.greenpenguin.co.uk

MIX
Paper from
responsible sources
FSC® C018179

Penguin Random House is committed to a
sustainable future for our business, our readers
and our planet. This book is made from Forest
Stewardship Council® certified paper.

This book is dedicated to all the Chibok Girls,
and to all victims of the Boko Haram insurgency.

CONTENTS

Chibok

Part One

Professor Americana

The town lay about a mile ahead, hidden behind rocky hills and baobab trees. There was still one more checkpoint to pass before we entered Chibok. We had left Maiduguri early and spent the night in Yola. The regular route from Maiduguri to Chibok, which passed through Damboa and normally takes two hours, was still in the hands of Boko Haram, and so we had to divert through Damaturu in Yobe State, and then to Gombe in Gombe State, getting to Yola in Adamawa State by night-fall—a detour of almost 500 miles.

We left Yola at 10:00 in the morning. This was the coolest it ever gets in these parts, with temperatures falling to the low fifties Fahrenheit at night. It was January, the middle of the season of Harmattan, a wind that blows in from the Sahara, carrying with it dust from the great desert. The fine sand particles go right into your nostrils and eyes, dehydrate the skin, crack the lips, and induce coughing fits

16   and general discomfort. Among the villagers, who mostly
go about in slippers or barefoot, the Harmattan cuts deep
grooves in their heels. Despite rolling up the windows, the
dust still managed to get into the car. All the way from Yola it
had clouded the windshield and piled up on the seats and on
our clothes and hair.

The closer we got to Chibok, the more checkpoints we
encountered. At each stop we had to get out of the car and
open the trunk; sometimes the soldiers went through our
bags, sometimes they just waved us through. As we passed
through Askira-Uba, the last local government area before
Chibok, signs of the ongoing battle between Boko Haram and
the military became more evident. Burned tanks and military trucks stood at the roadsides, rusting away. There were
houses with caved-in roofs and walls pockmarked by bullet
holes. There was a destroyed bridge around which we had to
detour.

Abbas, my guide, was driving. With us was Michael, a
member of the civilian Joint Task Force—local hunters and
youths working as volunteers alongside the military. He was
from Abbas's hometown and somehow related to him. We
had picked him up on the way, at Lassa junction, where he had
waited for us, seated on his bike with only his Dane rifle for
company. He had left the bike there and entered the car. When
I asked him if the bike was safe there in the bush by itself, he
said yes.

"Are you sure?"

He nodded. He appeared to be a man of few words. I was conscious of him seated right behind me, his rifle pointing in the general direction of my head.

The JTF was a coalition of the different branches of the armed forces formed on an ad-hoc basis to fight the insurgency. Civilian vigilantes knew the terrain better than the soldiers, who were mostly from distant parts of the country and didn't even speak the local languages. Nevertheless the civilian JTF's prowess in fighting Boko Haram had been much exaggerated and mythologized—for instance, they were believed to possess charms and medicines that made them invulnerable to bullets, and even invisible to the enemy during battle.

Michael was supposed to ease our passage through the checkpoints. And sure enough, after bringing on this new passenger we had passed two checkpoints unharassed; the soldiers only nodded at Michael and waved us through—his tan uniform and the gun seemed to be doing the trick. Until we reached one where we seemed to have passed a flag without stopping. As we passed a second flag we noticed a soldier under a tree by the roadside shouting and waving at us to stop, his gun pointed at our car.

"We thought we were clear to pass . . ."

Another soldier, a superior, came out of a house behind the tree. He was putting on a shirt and his skinny chest was

18   exposed momentarily. "You think? You think?" he shouted as he joined the others. "You people think we are here to play? I dey here for this bush fighting Boko Haram for two years now. Two years I no see my family, and you tell me you think?"

Thinking was clearly not allowed. He was almost shaking with anger, shouting at the top of his voice. I was glad he had no gun. "You better go and talk to him," I told Michael. There was another car next to ours; a man and the driver stood wordlessly beside the car, listening to the soldiers' rants. They were obviously in a similar situation as we were. Michael went to the soldier with the gun and showed his ID card.

"So you are civilian JTF? So what? Four months we have been here without salary, our friends are killed by Boko Haram, and I am sick. Four months no pay. And you tell me you think. You will see. I go keep you here for hours in this sun."

He let us go after about 15 minutes.

Checkpoints, or roadblocks as they are also commonly called, are a regular feature of road travel in Nigeria. Nigerians have become resigned to them the way they are resigned to the lack of reliable electricity or running water. Ostensibly, the roadblocks are there for enforcing traffic laws and ensuring travelers' safety, but in reality they are nothing but extortion points. They have become a place where you paid your taxes at gunpoint, fully knowing the taxes would not get to the state coffers but into private pockets. Since the Nigerian government placed most of the northeast region of the country under emergency rule in 2013, the roadblocks have proliferated. In some places they have become almost like settlements, humming with beggars, idlers, and boys and girls—out of school due to the insurgency—selling water and food to travelers. In Borno and Yobe states, the epicenter of the Boko Haram insurgency, there were roadblocks at about every two-mile interval. Before the insurgency the blocks were manned by policemen who'd chat with you about the weather or about the traffic as you handed them their bribe. They'd even give you change if you had no small notes; all very civilized. Now the checkpoints were guarded by scowling, uncommunicative soldiers in full war gear. I almost laughed when I saw a sign warning drivers that it is illegal to give bribes at checkpoints, with a phone number to call if a soldier solicited a bribe. This was the face of the new government of Muhammadu Buhari, who was elected in May 2015 on the promise to wipe out corruption and Boko Haram. Abbas told me he had tried the numbers and they didn't work.

At the checkpoints passengers in private cars were sometimes allowed to remain in their vehicle, but passengers in commercial vehicles had to get out and approach the soldiers on foot. Often male passengers had to take off their shirts and raise their hands as they passed the soldiers—Boko Haram insurgents sometimes detonated suicide vests at checkpoints. As the passengers passed they presented

20   their ID cards to the soldiers, who compared them to pictures of the 100 most-wanted Boko Haram members prom-
inently displayed at every checkpoint. Abubakar Shekau, the
Boko Haram leader, was ranked number 100; his enlarged
face with its signature leer occupied the center of the poster.
A few faces on the list had already been captured. Recently,
Khalid Al-Barnawi, the head of Ansaru (full name: Jamā'tu
Anāril Muslimīna fī Bilādis Sūdān, or "Vanguard for the Pro-
tection of Muslims in Black Lands"), a Boko Haram splinter
group responsible for the kidnapping and killing of many
foreigners, had been caught in a hideout in Lokoja, Kogi
State. One other reason ID cards were checked was because
Boko Haram members never carried them; to them they are
a Western invention and therefore haram, or forbidden. I
asked Abbas, would anyone without ID be arrested for a Boko
Haram member? No, not always. It mostly depended on the
discretion of the soldiers, on the answers the defaulter gave;
usually the punishment was a fine of anything between 200
naira to 500 naira.

Ahead of us was the last checkpoint before Chibok. This
was the most important checkpoint of all. The soldiers here
would determine whether I got to enter Chibok or not. Vehicles coming in or going out were given a special pass, which
they must present to the soldiers. Traders bringing sup-
plies from neighboring towns must have an inventory listing
every single item they carried. Since the kidnapping of over

276 schoolgirls in April 2014, and the subsequent media focus on the families of the kidnapped girls, the government had placed the town on lockdown. Journalists in particular were personae non grata. I was told of a British reporter who came as a guest of the wife of a local pastor and was turned back at this checkpoint.

The Chibok native, Reverend Titus Pona, chairman of the Christian Association of Nigeria, Borno State chapter, had promised that a local pastor would wait for me at the checkpoint and take me in as his guest. When I got the pastor on the phone, he made excuses and said he couldn't meet me. Now my fate rested on the mood of the soldiers. Abbas, whose hometown, Lassa, was only about thirty minutes from Chibok, said he had lots of friends here, and concocted a new story: We were coming from Lassa to visit his friends, one of whom had just gotten married. And there was the taciturn Michael of the JTF as backup if the new story failed.

And so, once more we got out of the car and approached the soldiers who were seated under a giant tamarind tree by the roadside. With them were three civilian JTF members with their Dane guns and knives tied on ropes around their waists. Michael identified himself and handed over his ID card. Next, Abbas handed over his driver's license and mentioned the name of his friend who we were ostensibly visiting. The soldier gave a noncommittal nod and turned to me. I handed over my State of Virginia driver's license.

"America," he said.

"I am Nigerian," I said. "But I live in America."

"Mistah Americana," he said.

"Actually, it's more like Nigeriana," I said, not sure where this was going. But he seemed suddenly to relax. The other soldiers were laughing and echoing, "Americana." Now I noticed how young they were: None of them could have been over twenty-five. They were just kids, sent here to fight a brutal enemy who relished capturing soldiers alive and slaughtering them like rams for propaganda videos. They were clustered around the one holding my driver's license, taking turns looking at it. The mood had lifted.

"So, what do you do in America?"

"I teach," I said. "I am a professor."

"Ah, Professor Americana." I laughed with them. Professor Americana. Why not. He returned my license and waved us through.

Checkpoints weren't only for regulating traffic—they also controlled the flow of the narrative surrounding the kidnapping. Propaganda was an important part of the war against Boko Haram, and the government wanted to ensure its version of events was always the definitive one. In December 2015, seven months after his election, President Buhari had gone on the BBC and declared a "technical" victory over Boko Haram. His information minister, Lai Mohammed, backed up the president's claim by leading a group of thirty-three journalists to parts of Borno State retaken by the military, as proof of Boko Haram's imminent defeat. He said the military had "so degraded the capacity of Boko Haram that the terrorists can no longer hold on to any territory just as they can no longer carry out any spectacular attack." This claim was received with skepticism.

In a move clearly calculated to undermine the government's claim, Boko Haram launched a series of spectacular attacks a few days later. Two suicide bombers struck a market in the town of Madagali in Adamawa State, killing more than twenty-five people. In neighboring Maiduguri several attacks killed more than thirty people and injured over a hundred. Although the Buhari government's claim was partly true—the group had been significantly degraded, and most of its captured territory had been retaken—most observers knew it'd take many years to defeat the group.

One of the defining characteristics of the group has been its special talent for resurrection, particularly after crushing defeats.

Jama'atu Ahlis Sunna Lidda'awati Wal-Jihad, or "the People Committed to the Propagation of the Prophet's Teachings and Jihad," was founded by the cleric Mohammed Yusuf, who followed Saudi Arabia's fundamentalist Salafist doctrine and called for the overthrow of the secular Nigerian government. Boko Haram is the group's nickname, and

24   very loosely translates to "Western education is abhorrent,"
     a centerpiece in Yusuf's teachings. Around 2002 he set up a
     complex in Maiduguri; his group was rather unremarkable
     during its first years of existence, despite Yusuf's claims
     of ties to Al-Qaeda, his increasingly militant teachings,
     and reports that his followers were stockpiling weapons in
     preparation for jihad. Tensions finally came to a head in July
     2009 when members of the group battled police and sol-
     diers in Maiduguri when they were stopped during a funeral
     procession for not wearing motorcycle helmets. Yusuf had
     found an excuse for an uprising, and launched attacks across
     five northern states. The government brutally put down the
     revolt after a few days, leaving more than a thousand dead
     and others captured. Troops surrounded Yusuf's compound
     and executed him. The government declared Boko Haram
     "crushed."

          That was not the case. The leadership simply went under-
     ground in various Salafi jihadist camps in Somalia, Sudan,
     Mali, and even as far away as Afghanistan, learning valuable
     terror techniques (including bomb making) which it would
     put to use a year later when Boko Haram reemerged under its
     new leader, Abubakar Shekau. Even more violent, remorseless,
     and unpredictable than Yusuf, Shekau typified the attitude of
     the resurgent terror group. In one of his propaganda videos in
     2012, he said, "I enjoy killing anyone that God commands me
     to kill, the way I enjoy killing chickens and rams."

Not much is known about Shekau except that he had married Yusuf's widow and adopted his children, symbolically taking over Yusuf's household and his mission. His video appearances show him cradling a Kalashnikov assault rifle, sometimes while sitting down in a room with a neutral background, sometimes strutting in front of war tanks and firing off shots, but always flanked by silent, well-armed lieutenants with faces covered. His speeches are mostly taunts at the Nigerian government, with threats toward Barack Obama, the West in general, and other world leaders thrown in almost at random, and pledges to kill whoever stands in the way of "Allah's mission." Ideologically, the group continued Yusuf's theological views, remaining completely against all forms of democracy (perceiving it as "a challenge to God's sovereignty") and insisting on sharia as the only acceptable code to live by.

Shekau's early efforts centered on prison breaks to free some of the Boko Haram members who had been arrested during the 2009 uprising. In September 2010, over 700 inmates were released in Bauchi. More followed in Maiduguri, Kano, Gombe, and other northeastern cities.

In June 2011, Boko Haram turned to suicide bombings, first targeting the Nigeria Police Force Headquarters in Abuja. The bomber, Mohammed Manga, a thirty-five-year-old well-to-do businessman who in his will left four million naira to his five children, was an early convert of Mohammed Yusuf.

26   Manga drove more than 500 miles from Maiduguri to Abuja
     overnight to target the Nigerian police boss Hafiz Ringim,
     who had earlier vowed to go after members of Boko Haram.
     Ringim wasn't killed, but the attack marked the first ever sui-
     cide bombing in Nigeria. Boko Haram claimed responsibility
     by having a spokesperson make a phone call to the media to
     provide them with information about the killer.

       A second suicide bombing followed in October, at the UN
     headquarters building in Abuja. A sedan loaded with explo-
     sives crashed through the gates of the compound and into the
     front doors before exploding, killing at least eighteen people.
     Until then, Boko Haram had focused their terror on local tar-
     gets; this was its first and still only high-profile attack on an
     international organization.

       Despite widespread condemnation, the U.S. State Depart-
     ment did not bother to place Boko Haram on its list of For-
     eign Terrorist Organizations. There were a number of reasons
     for this, one of which was the Nigerian government's refusal
     to cooperate with international organizations in the fight
     against Boko Haram. The U.S. would not designate the group
     "FTO" for another two years, following a spate of bombings in
     late 2013 that demonstrated the group's increased abilities to
     wreak havoc. The targets now included hospitals, churches,
     mosques, and markets. Boko Haram would often announce
     publicly beforehand the time of the attack and the target:
     They believed victory or loss came from God, and no power

could stop them unless God willed it. Announcing their plans in advance was a test—and proof of the justness of their cause.

To raise funds, they raided banks, mostly in rural areas, hauling away millions of naira, which they used to sponsor their insurgency. The group also tried to capitalize on existing tensions between Christians and Muslims in Jos and other parts of northern and central Nigeria, hoping to provoke a full-scale war between the two religions by bombing churches and killing hundreds of Christians.

At the height of its power, Boko Haram controlled over 70 percent of Borno State and many other areas in neighboring states. With the annexing of towns and villages, the group's ambition had expanded; it was now intent on establishing a Caliphate, ISIS style. This ambition wasn't idle, and the group made rapid advances, routing the military in Borno, Adamawa, and Yobe states. By 2015, it controlled twenty out of the twenty-seven local government areas in Borno State. The emir of Gwoza, one of the major emirates in Borno State, was killed by the sect, and they declared the town their caliphate's headquarters. It was an ideal location, in terms of defense, high up in the mountainous region near the Cameroonian border in northeastern Nigeria.

Boko Haram professes links to foreign terrorist organizations like Al-Qaeda in the Islamic Maghreb, and more recently, ISIS, after Shekau pledged his allegiance to the group

28   in a 2015 video. But apart from leading to a brief name change
to the Islamic States of West Africa, and a noticeable improve-
ment in the quality of its propaganda videos, it didn't amount
to much in terms of material support.

By 2013, the administration of President Goodluck Jonathan, which had responded indifferently to the Boko Haram
threat since his election in 2010, finally began to take the
fight more seriously. A state of emergency was declared
in the northeastern states of Borno, Adamawa, and Yobe.
Troops were mobilized and sent to the war front; Boko Haram
responded by changing its tactics, looking for even softer
targets.

On February 25, 2014, about fifty Boko Haram insurgents
invaded the Federal Government College, a coeducational secondary school, in the town of Buni Yadi in Yobe State. They
came in pickup trucks at around 9:00 at night, and threw
explosives into the boys' dorm rooms, then shot and stabbed
the boys as they tried to escape. Meanwhile, they rounded up
the girls, lectured them on the "evils of Western education,"
ordered them to get married, burned down the school buildings, then left. They didn't touch the girls, but fifty-nine boys
were murdered in cold blood.

Buni Yadi looked like a rehearsal for Chibok two months
later. This time there were no boys to kill, and the girls were
simply taken. As the government troops pushed Boko Haram
further into the forest, ransom payments became an easier

way to raise money, and kidnappings had already become more frequent. Boko Haram fighters also needed children and older women to cook and clean for them, and the younger women became "wives"—sex slaves and mothers to the next generation of fighters. Men too old to be conscripted were simply lined up against the wall and shot.

Chibok became the most symbolic of all the kidnappings, especially because the girls were under the care of the government when they were taken. The war against Boko Haram would never be won until the victims were at least accounted for. The government understandably continues to restrict access to Chibok town, and I was lucky to get in at all.

We climbed up a narrow dirt road past what looked like a military camp to our right, and suddenly we were inside Chibok. The dirt road cut through the tiny town like a river and exited at the other end; to the left of the road at the edge of town stood the Government Secondary School. The heart of the town was the marketplace. As in most African towns, the market was more than just a place for buying and selling. It is the town's social center. To get to one part of Chibok from another part one must pass through the market square, and in the course of the day almost everyone in town passes through the market at least once.

Since the kidnapping, the market has been dominated by soldiers patrolling or loitering on foot and in trucks; a

30   pickup filled with vigilantes bearing their trademark Dane
        guns was parked in front of a store. There were individual vig-
        ilantes standing in storefronts or passing by on foot or on
        bikes. Everybody rode bicycles, men and women and boys and
        girls. Motorbikes have been outlawed since the kidnapping,
        since they were Boko Haram's vehicle of choice, and anyone
        riding one could be suspected for a Boko Haram member and
        arrested, if he was lucky, or shot, if he wasn't. Four telecom
        masts towered over the market square, but ever since the kid-
        napping only one of them worked. Electricity, which came
        from the Damboa grid, had been cut off by Boko Haram for
        years. There was no running water—all day men and women
        pushed carts filled with yellow jerry cans through the narrow
        labyrinths between the mud houses, carrying water from
        wells. A Union Bank branch was closed, like most other ser-
        vices, and the building itself was crumbling.

        Chibok is perhaps the poorest and most neglected of all
        the twenty-seven local government areas in Borno State. The
        2006 census placed the population at around 66,000. Most of
        the people were farmers and hunters, although many younger
        men and women occupied mid-level positions in teaching, the
        military, and the civil service. The Chibok people call them-
        selves the Kibaku, which is also the name of the language they
        speak. The various clans and groups making up the Kibaku had
        been driven to the Chibok hills by Fulani jihadists and slave
        raiders in the nineteenth century, and they have remained here

ever since. Chibok is predominantly Christian in a predominantly Muslim state—the Chibok local government chairman is the only Christian among the twenty-seven local government chairmen in Borno State. It is a sleepy, dusty town where nothing ever seems to happen, and it would have continued its peaceful and obscure existence but for the event of April 14, 2014.

The Day They Took the Girls

My first task in Chibok was to find the local pastor who was supposed to meet me at the checkpoint. Soon I found the Reverend Philip Madu sitting inside his house, which was made of unplastered and unpainted red mud, like most houses here. Madu is the chairman of the Christian Association of Nigeria in Chibok, and head pastor of the Good News Evangelistic Ministry, one of the many churches in town. Another denomination, the Church of the Brethren in Nigeria, was however the largest in the state, with a congregation of over 100,000. It is an offshoot of the international Church of the Brethren, which, like the Quakers and the Mennonites, is pacifist. Nevertheless, it's been the denomination most affected by Boko Haram attacks.

The Reverend looked to be in his forties, of medium build and height, and he was dressed in the customary *kaftan* robe. He explained that he couldn't be at the checkpoint because he had been in a meeting, but I didn't care about the close call, as I had made it into Chibok. I was interested in something else. "Tell me about the night of the kidnapping," I began.

"Before that night, these things have been happening in neighboring villages, kidnappings and killings. In Kwaga close by, in one Sunday they killed over fifty Christians. In other neighboring villages as well. They burned down houses and killed people. Until it got to us on the fourteenth of April, 2014.

"Around 5:30 p.m. to 6:00 p.m. that day, I had a call saying there were rumors that they were coming to attack Chibok."

"Who called?"

"I got different calls, not one. That day my wife wasn't around, just the children and me. Well, around 10:00 p.m. or quarter to 11:00 p.m., I heard pa-pa-pa-pa, gunshots. I woke up the kids. We were sleeping out here in the yard. It was April and very hot. We heard the gunshots, going on and on. We ran out of town and hid behind the Bible school over there. [The attack] went on for hours. They started around 11:00 p.m.; they didn't finish until around 2:00 a.m.

"What happened affected me directly. They took two of my brother's daughters. My brother—same father, same mother. Up to now we haven't received any news of them. A few of the girls of course were able to run away from the abductors. I interviewed them. What they said is the same in all cases. When the men came to their hostel, they told them they were

34 soldiers. They told the girls, 'These people [Boko Haram] have come and we are here to protect you, so don't run, stay in one place.'

"They gathered them in one place. Then they marched them out of the school gate to the waiting cars. There was a truck they had seized; it had brought grains to the market. They took down the grains and put the girls in the truck and other small cars and pickups, according to the girls. They took the road toward Damboa, you will pass a village on the right, called Mboa, and the road goes to the right and leads all the way to Sambisa Forest.

"We of course didn't know what was going on. They went into town and burned down a few shops, including the house of the local council chairman, and another man living in Maiduguri. In some shops they took foodstuff. In the school they took foodstuff from the store and burned down some classes and hostels.

"Well, in the morning the news spread. When we went to the school we saw the girls' clothes and uniforms scattered all over the place. Parents started crying, but there was nothing they could do. There was no word from the government or any person in authority. The next day the parents said they just couldn't sit still and do nothing while their girls were being taken away. They said they'd rather die pursuing them.

"The men formed a group and went after them. They entered the bush and got to a village in Damboa that local government called Njaba, when the villagers saw them. They asked them if they were the parents of those girls, and they said yes. They said, 'These men are not too far ahead of you, but our advice is we don't think you will come back alive if you keep following them. What is the point in losing your life as well as that of your daughters? Better go back.' The parents went back."

"What of the military, no sign of them?" I asked

"No, not a word. And that was how it happened. And until today there is no sign or word about these girls. Of course a few of them jumped out of the truck, some had gone all the way to Sambisa Forest before escaping. God made a way for them and they escaped: They met some Fulani shepherds who hid them and helped them find their way back. But the rest of them, the majority, until today, no solid steps have been taken by anyone to bring them back. This April it will be two years. Well, that was the event of April 2014.

"They [Boko Haram] came back again, November 13, 2014. I remember, we were in church that day, me and my wife and my three small children. Around 3:45 p.m., we were having our Bible study. We heard the gunshots, this time they were coming from Askira, this same Mbala road you took to come today, and they were coming toward Chibok.

"We heard the gunshots, *pa-pa-pa-pa-pa*. The thirteenth of November, 2014. Well, the good thing is that we were still able to use motorbikes at the time. The church members stood up to leave, but I told them, 'No, lets pray first and ask for

36 God's guidance.' After prayer, before I could lock the church doors, bullets had started flying everywhere. We took the bike and started for the bush, toward Mife. I told my wife to climb on with the children, but she said, 'No, you men are more in danger, I hear they don't kill women. You go. I'll be fine.' We went to Mife, and from there to Bolakle."

At Bolakle he and the children were able to hitch a ride in a car to Damboa, and the next day they went on to Gombe, then on Saturday to Maiduguri. In Maiduguri they got the news that soldiers had beaten back Boko Haram and retaken Chibok. They returned to Chibok on Tuesday, but the children couldn't sleep at night because the soldiers were randomly firing gunshots every night to warn off the insurgents. Many who came back decided to leave again.

"Was your church attacked?" I asked.

"No, it was a miracle. They went into the church and they didn't touch anything. Instead they were playing the musical instruments all night long. That was what people told me. They said they could hear the drums from where they were hiding. The only thing they destroyed was a picture on the wall, a picture I brought back from Jerusalem in 2007."

"What of the parents of the kidnapped girls? How are they coping?"

He sighed and shook his head. "It is sad. A few of them have died. They developed high blood pressure and all sorts of ailments."

"Do you have hope the girls will be back?"

He was quiet for a while. Then he took a deep breath. "We put our trust in God. We don't trust in people or any power. If God has plans for them to return someday, they will return."

In order to speak to some of the parents of the victims, I had connected with Ruth from the International Organization for Migration. She was one of five locals trained as support workers pending the return of the girls. I was struck by how everyone here was careful to talk of *when*, not *if*, the girls came back.

Ruth was a teacher by training, and had herself gone to Chibok Girls Secondary School ten years ago. Recently married, she was heavily pregnant. Her husband was a pastor with one of the Pentecostal churches in Chibok.

"What are you supposed to do with the girls when they return?" I asked her. Counseling, she told me, and it would depend on the condition the girls returned in, what their needs were. In the meantime, she had grown close to the families of the victims, and some would stop by just to talk to her about their girls. It was getting dark already. The town had been under curfew ever since the kidnapping in 2014. No one, apart from the vigilantes, was allowed out at night until 7:00 in the morning. Defaulters were handed over to the soldiers, who decided what manner of punishment to mete out to them. But the military themselves did not go on patrol, though I was

38   assured they were camped up in the hills, about 500 in all, watching the village and monitoring all moving vehicles. John, Abbas' taciturn friend, told me not to worry too much about the curfew; he was an occasional member of the vigilante, like most youths in Chibok.

We drove to one of the parents' house, without headlights to avoid being spotted by the soldiers in the hills. The town's narrow and dusty streets were already empty except for a few children running about.

Yana Galang was waiting for us. Holding a flashlight, she led us to a small clearing in front of her house, where we sat down on low stools and logs. Her older daughter, Kulu, sat next to us with a child strapped to her back.

Yana, one of the leaders of the parents' association, had just returned from the capital, Abuja, where she had gone to see Muhammadu Buhari. I had read of the meeting in the newspapers, the first between the new president and the parents. It was a closed-door meeting, and the parents had been asked not to talk about it. The papers said the president had renewed his pledge to continue the search for the missing girls.

I asked her to recreate that day for me, but as she spoke, it struck me that she had repeated this story many times before—to the media, NGOs, Nigerian security agents, and many more. I wondered if the words carried the same weight and pain each time she repeated them. It seemed cruel to be asking her to relive that day.

"My daughter, Rifkatu, was not feeling well that day. She had had an appendix removed not too long before that day. She hadn't been going to school throughout the second term because of that. But because of the exam, she said it was best to go and stay in the hostel and to study with her classmates. She came home that weekend to collect a few things, and was going back on Monday, the fourteenth, the night they were taken.

"She went to her father and said, 'Baba, I am going back to school.' And he said, 'Let me drop you in the car.' I was seated right here at the time. She got her things together, soap and foodstuff, and her father asked her if she needed anything more. And she said yes, she needed *garri* [dried and ground cassava] and sugar. So, he took out a thousand naira note and gave her. She went to the market and bought *garri*, sugar, and Macleans [toothpaste]. She brought back a change of 400 naira and her father said, 'Keep it since you are going back to school. You will need it.' She said, 'Thank you.'

"Then she put down the bag with the things she bought right here, by this mortar, and went to get her friend in the neighboring house so they could go together. They were best friends and inseparable. She went through that tiny opening, running. She was wearing her uniform already. Her father came out looking for her and I told him she had gone to get her friend. Soon they came back, together with another girl who had come from a neighboring village and had spent the night

40   at Rifkatu's friend's house. And so they all went in the car to
the school. That was on Monday.

"I remember there was a wedding that day, and we had all
gone there and joined in the festivities. We were dancing all
evening and came back late. Around 10:35. So, that night we
were sleeping with the children outside in the yard, because it
was very hot. We heard the shots. I woke up. I was only dressed
in my wrapper, nothing else. I called out to my co-wife,
Emma's mum. I said, 'Mama Emma, these people have entered
our town. What should we do?'

"I left the small children and ran to my older son's room
and woke him up. He was wearing a white shirt. I told him to
take it off and wear something dark so he wouldn't stand out. I
came back to get the two younger children. At that moment
suddenly all the strength left my body. I felt weak. I couldn't
walk. I told them to go on and I'd come behind, but the older
boy said he couldn't leave me there. I told him, 'Just go.' We
had reached over there, near that neem tree. They went on.
I was wearing only my wrapper. I managed to follow other
people through the rocks under the hill, by the burial ground.
When we stopped there people told us we must move on, and
we climbed up on to the hill.

"We sat there, and each time I heard the gunshots my
stomach would turn and I had to go into the bush to defecate.
This went on until around 4:00 a.m. At some point my boy
came to me and said, 'Here, take my shirt.'

"In the morning we went back home. . . . I wanted to wash my face and pick out the thorns that had lodged in my feet while we were running, but I didn't have the energy to do it. I was so restless. I decided to go to my father's house to see how they were. I found my father lying down. The first thing he asked me was about my daughter at school. I told him they must be all right, surely they'd have ran off into the hills like everybody else. He looked at me and said, 'Are you sure?' He gave a deep sigh. He had already heard about the kidnapping but didn't want to say it out loud.

"At that moment my stomach turned suddenly and I felt like going to the toilet again, but I held it. I went back home and as I got there I saw my husband's brother coming toward me on his motorbike. He was shouting and crying as he came. And I thought, 'Someone has died.' He dropped the bike like this on the ground and said, 'Better if they had burned down the whole town than what they have done to us. They have taken all the girls at G.G. ["government girls" school].

"I started screaming, and I felt as if my life would come out. I called to their father who was sleeping inside the house. I started running toward the school, screaming and running. I felt as if my world had ended. They met me on the way, and took me on a bike to the school. That was it. The girls were gone. That is what happened.

"For two weeks after, I couldn't eat or sleep. I'd put food in my mouth and then throw it out again. I would go to the

42 toilet but nothing would come out. I would walk up and down, thinking. Two weeks. I couldn't sleep. But . . . only God knows what will happen. Our trust is in God."

"Have you heard of anything, news of the girls?"

"No. Nothing. And if anyone tells you anything, it is only lies. . . . I believe though, that someday, something will happen. I don't know how, maybe through one of the girls, someone who truly believes in God. He will use one of them to do something. I believe that."

"What of the few that escaped. Did they tell you anything?"

"The ones that returned, they fell off the truck as they were being taken. . . . I've talked to them. We went to Lagos to raise awareness about the kidnapping with some of them; three of them are now in America. According to what they told us, they had gone all the way into Sambisa Forest. Their car was the very first to get to the forest. They were crammed into the trunk of the car. When they got there, the men gave them a mat to sit on. And they said, no, they'd sit on the bare ground, and the men said, 'Why, are you annoyed at us?' They said no, they'd just rather sit on the ground. Four of them decided to run. They said they'd rather die trying to escape and be eaten by animals than stay with these men.

"One of the men heard them talking and said, 'Hey, what are you talking about?' They kept quiet. They decided to tell the man they wanted to go into the bush to urinate. When they told him that, he said they should do it right there. But

they said no, in their tradition a woman wasn't allowed to pee
in front of a man. They said they were shy. And so he agreed,
but he didn't let them go far. They pressed him, saying, '*Allah
ngubro* [Kanuri language meaning *sir*], we really can't go with
you here looking at us.' He said, 'Okay, but don't go far.' And
they went into the bush and continued walking. The fourth
girl didn't go with them, she even threatened to report them to
the man. But they kept on walking, holding hands.

"As they went further into the bush they encountered
Boko Haram sleeping under trees, tired from the raid, and they
took a different path. Three times they encountered them, and
they had to take another route. But they didn't turn back. They
came upon a Fulani woman who took them in and gave them
clothes to wear. They took off their school uniform and put on
the clothes the Fulani woman gave them. She gave them food
and warm water, and she led them to Damboa.

"That's how they escaped. A few others jumped off the
trucks as they went, clinging to tree branches and leaping off.
There was one who broke her leg and had to be nursed when
they came back."

She handed me a picture of Rifkatu, a pretty, wide-eyed
girl, staring straight at the camera in her Sunday best dress.

We were spending the night in another of Abbas's friends'
houses. His name was Foni. When I met him earlier in the
day he had been quiet and self-effacing. Now he was loud and

44   quite assertive, interrupting everyone with the same phrase, "Don't rush." He had been drinking in a dark and squalid beer joint when we picked him up on our way from Yana Galang's house. I was so surprised to see a beer joint in Chibok, given the somber mood that hung over the town, that I had to go in to see what it looked like. There wasn't much to see. There was a dirty white plastic table with plastic chairs arranged in the middle of the compound. Four men, including Foni, sat talking in undertones with green bottles of beer before them, occasionally calling out to the barman who came out to refresh their drinks, counting his money and giving change with the light from a flashlight.

Foni's home was the kind of house one expected to see in an upscale neighborhood in Maiduguri or Abuja. It was a spacious bungalow with a rather extensive verandah over the front entrance. Young fruit trees were growing all over the compound. There was a chandelier hanging from the ornate wooden ceiling in the living room. An arched doorway led from the living room to the kitchen. The house belonged to Foni's older brother. His picture stood over a television set against the wall. He had a strong and confident stare.

He was, like his brothers and their father before them, a successful businessman, and then had gone into politics. He ran for the state house of assembly under the People's Democratic Party, the dominant party in the state, and it looked like he was going to win. Then one night two gunmen came

to the family house where he was staying and shot him. Foni
and his younger brother, Peter, who were in another room in
the house, barricaded the door and made frantic phone calls
to the neighbors, but no one came. The gunmen shot through
the door, and it hit Peter in the abdomen. Foni, thinking his
younger brother was dead, hid in a corner. The gunmen broke
down the door and saw Peter on the floor, writhing and near
death. They stood over him, debating whether to finish him off
or to go. They decided there was no point in wasting more bullets on him, and they left.

"Did they get the killers?" I asked Abbas when he told me
the story.

"They had suspects. Foni recognized one of the voices,
and the man was arrested."

"Did they find out who sent them?"

"A rival politician. He was tried, and acquitted. There
wasn't enough proof."

Then Foni told us of Boko Haram's last visit to the village
in November 2014.

"I was here, right here in this room with my girlfriend.
On that couch. We heard shooting and I said to her, 'Ke, these
people are here.' She didn't believe me at first. She started to
argue. 'Don't rush,' I told her. 'Don't rush.' You see, in all sit-
uations you have to use your brain. Then the shooting got
louder, and she believed me. We ran out and we joined other
people escaping. We didn't take a single thing with us, we

46   just ran. We didn't even lock the doors. And you know what, it turned out to be a good thing. Because these people, wherever they encountered a locked door, they shot it down with a rocket launcher. *Boom!* That's what they did to every door they couldn't open."

"Did they destroy anything in the house?" I asked.

"Not a single thing. Two of them stayed here for two days before the military came. Oh, they took some of my clothes. They changed there in the bathroom and left their old clothes on the floor, all covered in blood. When I came back I took it out and I burned it in the backyard. They had searched in the kitchen, looking for food and for kerosene or petrol for their motorbikes, but they didn't touch anything else."

Peter, Foni's brother who was shot in the stomach, sat in the corner listening, chiming in once in a while.

For such a small town, Chibok abounded with stories of violence and assassinations, most of them related to religion or politics. There hadn't been elections in Borno State in a while because of the insurgency, so all local council chairmen were appointed by the state governor on a caretaker basis for a period of six months at a time. One local government chairman, Wanangu Kachiwa, was assassinated in 2012. The assassins came to his house and found no one at home, so they sat down at the gate and waited. It was a Sunday and Kachiwa was away at church with his family. A neighbor saw the suspicious looking men and tried to warn Kachiwa's daughter, but she had left her phone at home. When the family returned, the men followed them into the house—Kachiwa probably thought they were his constituents from Chibok who had come to ask for a favor—and as soon as they were inside they pulled out their guns and told Kachiwa they had been sent to kill him. They shot him in front of his wife and daughter and walked out. The papers said the men were Boko Haram members, but no one knew why they targeted the Chibok local council chairman.

A History of Violence

Nigeria is Africa's most populous country, with around 200 million people and over 400 ethnic groups, each speaking its own distinct language. As of 2015, Nigeria is the world's twentieth largest economy, with a GDP of more than $500 billion. The country is the seventh largest oil exporter in the world. Its people are among the most educated and enterprising on the continent. Despite this enormous potential, the nation's march to modernity remains mired in political disharmony and government dysfunction. Its history is filled with unsolved political assassinations, palace coups, and electoral thuggery.

Nigeria became independent in 1960, and compared to other British colonies like Kenya and Zimbabwe, the handover was peaceful, even cordial. Nigeria didn't have to fight a war of independence, and perhaps that is one reason the country's political elite remains disunited. Wars of independence often

forge a unity of purpose among a people and bring forth a   49
cadre of leaders tempered by the struggle—at least that's how
the theory goes.

Soon after independence Nigeria's ethnic and political disunity began to show. In 1966, just six years later, the
country experienced its first coup d'état in which almost the
entire crop of post-independence political leaders was wiped
out by young military officers, and the template had been set.
In 1967 the Igbos of Southeastern Nigeria attempted to secede,
declaring their region the Republic of Biafra; a civil war ensued
and took over a million lives, most of them civilian. General Yakubu Gowon, the military president who led the federal government during this time, was ousted in a palace coup
by Brigadier Murtala Muhammad, who was himself killed six
months later, by Major Buka Dimka. Dimka didn't get to be
president, though; he was court-martialed and executed by a
firing squad.

Muhammadu Buhari, the current democratically elected
president, also came from the military, and staged his own
coup in 1983, though his first bid in power lasted only two
years. He was ousted by General Ibrahim Babangida, who
ruled for nine years. Babangida's term was highlighted by
his execution of one of his best friends, General Mamman
Vatsa, on charges of yet another attempted coup d'état. He
also scuttled the 1992 elections, generally agreed to have
been won by millionaire Moshood Abiola. Babangida, in

50   a face-saving move, handed over power to a hastily put-together caretaker government chaired by businessman Ernest Shonekan, who, you guessed it, was promptly kicked out in another coup, by General Sani Abacha. Abacha gained infamy as the man who hanged environmental activist and author Ken Saro-Wiwa, but his list of state sanctioned thuggery and assassinations remain, to date, the benchmark in Nigeria's history. Nigeria's political history reads like something out of *I, Claudius.*

At the state level, governors keep private armies to intimidate the opposition and to ensure their own reelection and that of their associates. Bauchi State had the most unambiguously named private army of all, called Sara-Suka, meaning, "hack and stab."

At even lower levels the students and the masses vent their frustrations in religious violence, kidnappings, and robberies. The people copy their rulers, just as children ape their parents. Violence is a symptom of a dysfunctional system, where people have no patience for or confidence in due process. The poor don't believe they can get justice from the courts, because usually they can't; the elite know the system is rigged because they rigged it. The ones at the top keep the door shut because they don't want to share the spoils of office. Actual violence, or the threat of it, helps to keep the populace in check, just as poverty does. Keep the people scared and hungry, encourage them to

occasionally purge their anger on each other through reli-
giously sanctioned violence, and you can go on looting the
treasury without interference. I used to wonder why the
facilities at our airports and in almost all public buildings in
Nigeria were always broken and substandard, until I realized
it was not accidental. It is a way of controlling the masses.
The masses must never be allowed to think they deserve
standard service. Even if they get what is theirs, like decent
salaries, healthcare, and education, they must first grovel
and beg for it, so that when they finally get it they feel it
comes from the munificence of their political overlords, and
not as a right.

"I am a civil servant, I can lose my job if I talk to you," said Bula
Madu. A tall man, dressed in a loose, green *kaftan*, Madu was
one of the vice-principals of the Chibok Government Secondary School. It wasn't 8:00 a.m. yet but he was already at
the market, where we found him, seated in front of a cement
store listening to a transistor radio held close to his ear. Since
the closure of the school two years ago, he and the other
teachers and administrators of the school have found themselves underemployed.

Madu said he had strict instructions from the government not to talk to reporters. He wasn't even allowed to travel
outside Chibok without permission.

"Why?" I asked.

52   "I don't know. They don't want us to say the wrong thing. The girls are still missing. Everything is still under investigation."

Finally, he agreed to an interview, but under one condition: The PTA chairman must give his permission.

Madu and I found the PTA chairman seated on a mat in front of his house, not too far away from where Yana Galang lives. I told him who I was and we began to talk about the kidnapping when a car pulled up. We stopped talking as a man came out of the car and joined us on the mat. The chairman introduced the newcomer as an ex-police officer and one of the town's leading men. Then he introduced me and said I was writing a book on the Chibok kidnapping.

"You have to get clearance from the authorities," the man said. He had a way of leaving his mouth open even when he wasn't talking. Through his open mouth I could see his black, rotten teeth. That was the end of the interview. Madu looked apologetic, the chairman looked cowed, and the newcomer continued to look at me. So, I thanked them and left.

The staff of Chibok Secondary School hadn't had an easy time of it since the kidnapping. They had been summoned and questioned by the presidency and the state governor; a few editorials in the media had even suggested a conspiracy. Why, one of them questioned, did the principal allow the exams to continue when the exams board had directed all regional schools in Borno, Yobe, and Adamawa states to send their students to state headquarters and other big cities, where there was better security in place? Another vice principal had been accused of knowing about the raid beforehand, and was even said to have aided Boko Haram. On the day of the kidnapping, he had insisted that no girls should step outside the school, even though students were sometimes allowed to go home at the end of the day, because school was not in regular session. Surely, they reasoned, he must have wanted the girls to be taken by Boko Haram. But then, there was so much confusion surrounding the kidnapping, most of it arising from people's frustrations and a desire for easy answers and logic in what was clearly an illogical situation.

The Chief Imam of Chibok, Mallam Kyari, was much younger than I expected, definitely not yet forty. He apologized profusely for keeping us, he had been at a burial and had hurried back straight from there. He was wearing a traditional *babban riga* robe with *dan chiki* and cap. We were seated in his *zaure*—a staple feature of Hausa architecture, a room at the very entrance of the compound, with two doors, one facing the street, and one leading into the compound where only women and male family members are allowed to enter. All other men must stop at the *zaure,* where the father of the house usually receives them.

    Despite his relative youth, Kyari was already the father of the house, thanks to a Boko Haram raid in November 2014.

54   "That was their third coming. They came around 3:47 p.m., I remember the exact time because we had just finished praying in the mosque. At the time, my father, the Chief Imam, Allah bless his memory, was still alive. My father went on home, and I remained behind. The noise of their shooting was everywhere. And I thought to myself, these people are here, and when they take over a town, they just don't leave immediately. They stay for months, even years. In Gwoza they were there for about nine months. They even killed the emir of Gwoza.

"And we decided we couldn't stay. We must leave. At home I found my wife who told me the children had gone to the well to fetch water. I told her, 'You, start running toward Mife. I will go toward the well and gather the children. I went on my motorbike. But before going I went into the main house and told my parents we had to run, these people are killers and we can't wait for them to find us here. We all set out and I went on my bike to the well, but no one was there. The children weren't there. Only shoes and jerry cans and buckets strewn all over the place.

"And just then we saw their car coming. It was a pickup, and if they had wanted to kill us then, they could have. They were driving through very fast, and their target was the military camp. That was what saved us; they could have surely killed us.

"That night, we slept near a village called Kubumbula. We slept in an open farm, there must have been about a hundred

persons with us. In the morning some were saying, surely
they must have left by now. But others said, no, let's wait.
If they are gone, word will soon get to us. By 7:00 a.m., they
started shooting again. We could hear them. I was thinking
about my wife and my children. I hadn't seen them since I left
home.

"I decided to go look for them. First I had to get fuel for my
bike. I headed toward Kubumbula, following the *burtali* [cow
trail]. In Kubumbula I met my brothers and sisters, so many
people, but none of them had seen my wife or children. I went
on to Mife—there I met my wife, but not the children. We were
told they were in another village, Gaglan. I took my wife on the
bike and we went on to Gaglan.

"On the way, I met an elder, a good friend of my father's.
The first thing he told me was, 'Have you heard about your
father?' I said, 'No.' He said, 'Well, you father fell while running.
His blood pressure rose and he collapsed.' He said my younger
brother had gone to Gaglan to look for me. So, I went into
Gaglan and met my brother, Bana, there. He told me our father
fell, just after Chibok, before Gaglan. They were together with
my sisters, and a friend of his; they tried to pick him up, but
they couldn't and had to leave him there.

"They described the exact location where they left him
and I said, 'Well, how can we go there now?' Bana and one of our
cousins decided to go back on a bike; halfway they left the bike
and continued on foot. They found him where he had fallen

56   and put him on the bike. It was a big bike, all three of them rode on it. When I saw them I didn't know he was dead. But when I touched him, his body was cold. He had been dead for a while. And so we told the people of Gaglan the Chief Imam was dead and we had to bury him right there. There was no time to waste.

"We gathered together some of the people from Chibok and some local Gaglan people. I asked around if anyone had a plain white cloth so we could wrap the body with it. But it wasn't easy. The people of Gaglan had taken most of their belongings into the hills and hidden them when they heard the shooting. Luckily, one old man had a plain white cloth and he offered it to us. He described where he had hidden his belongings and his son went on a bike and brought it. We buried the Chief Imam there. It was a Friday, early in the morning."

"The only thing it is okay to kill are animals, and only for food. If you are not going to eat it, don't kill it. How then can you kill a man, who is just like you, with hands and feet and life just like yours, who has done nothing to you, you never knew him or met him before, how can you question his existence, and even kill him? In Islam, any man who kills another man, with no just cause, he should also be killed.

"They now even kill other Muslims, they throw bombs in mosques while people are praying. Islam doesn't sanction that. This is just a sect with its own doctrine and its own way of thinking, but it is not Islam."

Although I had never met the late Chief Imam, I somehow imagined him to be like Mallam Audu, who ran a Koranic school not too far away from my childhood home in Gombe. The mallam was old and was always seated in his *zaure*, his face buried in his Koran. We had to take our chickens to him to slaughter, otherwise our Muslim neighbors wouldn't eat our food. I was about ten years old, and the task of taking the chicken to the mallam always fell to me, and I'd sit outside the *zaure* and wait for him. When he found a suitable place to stop in his meditation, he'd walk out—I remember he had a limp—and I'd hand him the chicken. He'd pin it down, whisper a prayer, and cut its neck with his sharp knife, which he always took out of a skin scabbard, and we'd both watch the blood drain out of the chicken into a little groove in the dirt. After the blood had drained and the chicken had stopped twitching, he'd pour water over the chicken's severed neck and then hand it over to me. I'd pay him and leave.

At the front of his house were his *almajirai*, Hausa for Koranic students, who were always hunched over their wooden slates, reading loudly from the Koran. At night they'd make a bonfire from whose light they'd read. Sometimes Mallam Audu would walk out amongst them, whip in hand, laying into them when they appeared to be nodding off. Only when the fire had burned out were they allowed to go to sleep.

58   In the evening, at mealtime, the *almajirai* would stand with their bowls outside our door and sing, begging for food. They were mostly kids about my age, ten or even younger, sent by their parents to live with their teacher and learn the Koran by rote, until they mastered it. This was the traditional, pre-colonial way of learning in the north, when education meant Islamic education, and nothing else. A critique of the *almajiri* system in northern Nigeria is that unscrupulous teachers and politicians often turn these young boys into their private foot soldiers for their selfish ends. Many Boko Haram fighters were drawn from this pool.

But still, the version of Islam I grew up with was a tolerant Islam. I remember, in the month of Ramadan, after the break of fast in the evening, young Muslim men and women would go out in costume to perform plays in front of audiences, from house to house. The plays in these street theaters were mostly secular, from love stories to slapstick comedies, and could be elaborate with singing and crowd participation. This is one of my best memories of childhood.

That version of Islam was able to accommodate tradition and diversity, and didn't view the rest of the world through a puritanical lens. But all that changed, as if in a day. A stricter, less tolerant version of Islam emerged and took over the scene.

If one were to point to a single event in Nigeria's history that marked the rise of this age of intolerance, it would be the Maitatsine uprising of the 1980s. Named for its sect founder

Muhammadu Marwa, who was popularly known as Maitat-sine, meaning "one who curses" because of his penchant for shouting curses at "nonbelievers" while preaching. Marwa was originally from Cameroon, but had lived in the city of Kano on and off for decades and had amassed a large following among the poor, the many unemployed immigrants from Niger, Chad, and Cameroon, and the *almajirai*. Marwa was not only contro-versial but truly radical, as he denounced parts of the Koran, criticized the Prophet Muhammad, and even claimed to be a prophet himself.

Like Boko Haram after him, Marwa was opposed to most aspects of modernization and to all Western influence. He and his followers, known as 'Yan Tatsine, segregated them-selves from the rest of society, viewing anyone not belonging to their sect as an infidel and fair game for jihad. Throughout the 1970s the 'Yan Tatsine increasingly clashed with Nige-rian authorities, and in late 1980 the army finally stepped in, killing thousands, including Marwa himself. Hundreds fled Kano to seek refuge in neighboring villages and near Maiduguri, Kaduna, Yola, and Gombe. Riots would break out throughout the '80s, and Marwa's successor would not be captured until 2004. The Maitatsine was the first mass reli-gious uprising post-independence, and the Nigerian historian Toyin Falola has pointed out that it happened "against a back-drop of declining revenues, high unemployment rates, polit-ical corruption and rivalries, government mismanagement,

60   rampant materialism, and serious popular concern about the erosion of moral and religious values."

But this wasn't only happening in Islam. Christianity too was changing, even if not as violently. A frenzy of charismatic Christianity had taken hold in the southern cities, Lagos, especially. I lived in Lagos in 1999 when every morning our bosses would ask us to hold hands and sing and pray before start of work—and no, I wasn't working in a church, I was working for a media house. Coincidentally, or rather co-relatively, this was a time when our sales were dropping drastically. As the economy declined, and corruption became more rampant, people sought answers in religion. But an irrational reliance on religion, instead of giving the people peace and comfort, only made them less tolerant and more desperate.

We left Chibok at midday. The night before we had busted the car's exhaust pipe on an outcropping as we drove without headlights, so we had to take it to the shop. "Americana," the mechanic shouted as I approached. I recognized him even without his Dane gun or his knife hanging from his waist— he was one of the JTF soldiers at the checkpoint yesterday. He looked different in his mechanic's garb. He looked normal. This is how life was before Boko Haram, before the kidnappings, killings, and vigilantism transformed the country. Normal.

The road out of town to Damboa passed right in front of the secondary school. Soldiers at a checkpoint guarded the school entrance, and I asked if I could go in to take pictures, but the answer was no. We continued on the dusty road where mounds of sand were left along the side, as if someone had started work on it and then changed his mind. The lack of good roads in Borno State made it hard to fight Boko Haram, as almost all of them were untarred and impassable once the rainy season started in April. The militants, on the other hand, could traverse freely on foot or on their motorbikes.

This was the road they took the night of April 14, 2014, on their bikes and in pickup trucks. There had been a wedding that day, so there were many new faces in town, and any of them could have been Boko Haram. This road was also where they led the girls until they rendezvoused at a stop where twenty-five parked cars and trucks were waiting. One of the trucks was commandeered from the market, and the driver was forced at gunpoint to stay at the wheel. Along the way he had tried to encourage the girls to jump, and it was probably thanks to him that some escaped. A few of them were even able to get away after having been taken all the way to the terrorists' stronghold in Sambisa. There were fifty-seven escapees in all.

Some of the escaped girls eventually moved to America. Others remained in the country. I had asked Ruth, who had arranged my meeting with the mother Yana Galang, whether I could meet some of them. Unfortunately, the ones who were

62   still in the area were away at school in different parts of the
      region. The best time to see them was during the vacations,
      and the next one was Easter break in March. I would have to
      return.

Inside Boko Haram Heartland

Part Two

Gombe

Gombe was the halfway point between Chibok and Maiduguri. We had passed sleepy mud villages, all identical, with dust-covered children chasing plastic balls in the square and a few goats and chickens wandering about. In all the villages the school buildings—usually consisting of about two or three rectangular brick structures with zinc roofs, and a yard in the center—had been all burned down. This was a sure sign of Boko Haram's passage through the area. In some places we saw broken bridges, destroyed by Boko Haram to impede military pursuit. From Damboa junction to Biu we passed many ghost towns, village after village with no sign of people or livestock—only tall grasses growing inside the roofless houses and covering every available space in between the houses. The inhabitants had been chased off, or killed off, by Boko Haram.

It was therefore almost a shock to see the teeming population in Gombe. The pedestrians were congested by the roadsides and cars and bikes were honking and swerving and driving straight through the red traffic lights. Like other big cities in the northeast, Gombe had seen an influx of refugees from the rural areas. There were people from the border villages and towns in Borno and Adamawa states who had fled and were living with friends, family, or in internally-displaced-persons camps in Gombe. Those who still had jobs to go to commuted to work in their states, but lived in Gombe.

The town had been spared most but not all of Boko Haram's brutal attacks. There had been shootings at beer parlors, bomb explosions at bus stations, and a jail break at the town's central prison. On Feb 14, 2015, a convoy of Boko Haram militants attempted to break into the armory at the military barracks. It took hours of fighting, including aerial support from a fighter jet, to repel them. Before the terrorists left they distributed leaflets warning people not to vote in the presidential elections originally slated for that day, but which had already been postponed by the Jonathan government because of security concerns in the northeast.

This is where I grew up, in the 1970s and early 1980s. My earliest memories were made here. The Gombe Emirate was founded in 1804 at the start of the Fulani Jihad, a series of holy wars that saw the Fulani people oust the Hausa from power. Through the wars the military and spiritual leader Usman dan Fodio established the Sokoto Caliphate and brought about the

spread of Islam in most of northern Nigeria. His student, Buba
Yero, led the jihad in Gombe against the Jukun, who were then
the dominant power in the region. A Fulani emir was installed
over the mostly Hausa population. The conquered people
were converted to Islam.

   The Sokoto Caliphate was one of Africa's most powerful
empires at the time, with about thirty independent kingdoms
coming together in a loose confederacy. Gombe was one of the
jewels in the Sokoto Caliphate's crown. It is located where the
mainly Muslim upper north meets the significantly Christian
central north of Nigeria, a section of the country commonly
referred to as the "Middle Belt," a classification most Christian parts of northern Nigeria fall into culturally, if not geo-
graphically. The Sokoto Caliphate was an agrarian economy,
with a workforce based on slave labor, and most of the slaves
came from the "pagan" communities of the Middle Belt.
The Sultanate struck a deal with the British not to intro-
duce Western education or Christianity to the north as part
of its capitulation requests, but as soon as these communities were able to, they embraced both as a counter to, if not a
refuge from, jihadist invasions. The Caliphate could enslave
them, as they were non-Muslims. "The area became a virtual
slave farm," according to historian Toyin Falola. The people of
the Middle Belt "were derided as 'infidels' whom the Muslims
could tolerate as neighbors without having to choose between
offending Allah or converting them forcibly to Islam."

68   This region, often seen by outsiders, erroneously, as part
of a homogenous "north"— meaning any part of the country
above the River Niger-River Benue line and commonly viewed
as all Muslim and all Hausa Fulani—still has its many fault
lines. And because these divisions predated the birth of the
nation, most people here—and this is true to a large extent in
other parts of the country—are always Muslim or Christian
first, ethnic affiliation second, and Nigerian third.

The demography of Gombe, like that of most northern
cities, is subtly discriminatory. This is often never mentioned, but always exercised. Christians and non-indigenes
mostly reside in a part of town situated outside the walls of
the old city and away from the emir's palace. My family lived
there, in a large tenement compound of about seven families,
in which we were the only Christians. Looking back, I cannot
recall a single religious conflict between our Muslim neighbors and us.

But the 1970s was a period which most Nigerians old
enough to remember would perhaps regard as the country's
golden era. The civil war had ended and the country entered its
oil boom years. In 1974, under the recommendation of Jerome
Udoji, the former head of civil service, the government dou-
bled the salaries of all public servants, a move so popular it
was dubbed the "Udoji Award." The country was flush with
petro-dollars. General Yakubu "Jack" Gowon, then the head
of state, was reputed to have said to a foreign journalist that

money wasn't the problem, but how to spend it. Kleptoctracy
hadn't yet taken root as a principle of governance. The specter
of unemployment and youth restlessness had not yet reared its
head. Education from primary to university level was free for
all Nigerians, and this was the case until the late 1990s. Every
graduate was assured of a job. This was also the time when
Nigeria missed the chance to establish a solid foundation for
its economic future through industrialization. The government wasted money on mismanaged expenditures, typical of
which is the "cement armada" of 1975. Government agents had
signed contracts to deliver twenty million tons of cement a
year to Lagos, despite the fact that the port could handle only
one million tons per year. Hundreds of cement ships clogged
the harbor so badly that essential goods couldn't be unloaded.

The "cornering" of state money and privilege for personal
use became the norm. Ethnic and religious divisions, used so
successfully by the British during the colonial era to divide
and rule, resurfaced and were refined by the new elite, inher-
itors to the British colonial mantle. A once vibrant middle
class of civil servants, entrepreneurs, and university profes-
sors, trained by the British, would be gradually decimated and
sent into exile in America and Europe by successive military
dictatorships.

The Sokoto Caliphate, whose political power had been
reduced to ceremonial symbolism by the British and the Nigerian state, still wielded religious influence over Muslims, and

70   the propagation of Islam continued to be one of its primary
      duties. Ahmadu Bello, a scion of the Usman dan Fodio dynasty
      and first Premier of the Northern Region, sought to convert
      the "pagans" of northern Nigeria, if not the whole of Nigeria.
      Religious Muslims in the north contested the legitimacy
      of the secular Nigerian state. The Constituent Assembly of
      1979, elected to draft a new constitution in preparation for the
      nation's transition to a civilian government, came under pres-
      sure from Muslims who were uncomfortable with the term
      "secular" and ended up declaring Nigeria a "multi-religious"
      state. In 1999, Governor Ahmed Yerima of Zamfara State
      unilaterally opted for the sharia justice system, a move that
      many saw as a challenge to the southern Christian president,
      Olusegun Obasanjo. Soon the call for sharia in all northern
      states reached a groundswell. By 2012, all twelve northern
      states, including Kaduna, Niger, and Gombe, all of which have
      significant Christian populations, had declared sharia as the
      official state law.

          Northern Christians saw this unilateral adoption of sharia
      as just another act of marginalization in a series of many
      such acts. Their protests and complaints were met by plati-
      tudes from the state governors, assuring them that sharia was
      "optional" and applied only to Muslims. In states like Kano
      and Zamfara, the *hisbah*, or sharia police, openly harassed and
      closed down bar rooms and hotels, mostly ones owned by
      Christians.

Are all northern Muslims antagonistic toward Christians?
Certainly not. Yet many are aware of and complicit in the insti-
tutionalized bias that often places the Muslim indigene first
and the Christina indigene second in most things that matter,
like job promotions and political appointments. To most
northern Christians, this persistent, attritional "jihad" is
nothing but a continuation of what their parents went through
over a hundred years ago. The jihadist impulse, tamed by years
of experiment with democracy and encroaching modernity,
can still be whipped up and exploited by extremist elements
like Boko Haram.

And so when Boko Haram raided the school in Chibok and
took 276 young girls, and when its leader Abubakar Shekau
boasted in his propaganda video, "I took your girls. I will turn
your girls into slaves," the parents, descendants of the Middle
Belt "pagans," understood exactly what he was saying.

Maiduguri

Three days before my trip to Chibok I had flown into Maiduguri from Abuja. The flight had been delayed for over an hour due to bad weather. The Harmattan hung over Abuja and most of northern Nigeria in a white, soupy pall, cutting visibility to near zero. The weather is fickle and changes fast around this time of the year. By May, Maiduguri would get so intolerably hot that if you took a shower, before you left the bathroom the water on your body would have turned into sweat. But despite the swirling dust and the dehydrating wind, this was, weather-wise, the best time to come to Maiduguri. Because electricity and air-conditioning cannot always be guaranteed, better the Harmattan than the hellish heat. It gets so hot here, the joke goes, that you don't need to boil water to make tea—it comes out of the tap already boiling.

The invisible landscape below our plane was mostly Sahel savanna, the vegetation getting progressively thinner and drier as one leaves Abuja and enters Borno State in the northeast. Borno State is vast, covering 27,372 square miles, making it the second largest state in the country. It has the most international borders of any state, adjacent to Niger, Chad, and Cameroon.

In the heart of the state and running toward the southeast is the Sambisa Forest, which stretches from Borno State to neighboring Yobe, Gombe, Bauchi, and Kano. It is populated by thick-barked and thorny trees and bushes, which makes it hard to penetrate. A few hundred miles northwards the vegetation peters out into the Sahara. Southeastwards it meets the Mandara Mountains and the Gashaka Gumti National Park, which forms a corridor into the central African forest.

This is Boko Haram territory. If the group, which sprouted up organically in this region, were to randomly pick any terrain in the whole country for the best cover and the best bolt-holes, it couldn't have hit on a better place.

Abbas and I took a taxi into town from the airport. A reporter friend had told me what happened when he mentioned Boko Haram to a cab driver. He had arrived from Lagos and at the airport he had grabbed the first taxi he could find. Pressed for time and always conscious of his looming deadline, he had blurted out to the driver, "Can you take me to where I can meet Boko Haram members?" The car came to a screeching halt and the driver turned to him. "Don't ask me about Boko Haram. I don't know them. My agreement with you is to take you to your hotel, no more."

74   So I employed a less direct approach. "The last time I was in Maiduguri was over twenty years ago," I told the driver. "So much has changed."

Our driver, however, turned out to be rather garrulous, his Kanuri accented Hausa rising and falling with the cadence of his speech.

"Our problem is modernity," he said. "We accept modernity too quickly. Now a woman will go out with a foreigner, a white man. Before, our women would be too scared to go near a white man. Now, we spill our secrets to the white man, everything we know we go and tell him for reward, all in the name of Western education."

I was surprised by how close his words were to the general Boko Haram ideology. The words boko haram, after all, can be roughly translated as "Western education is abhorrent." There are of course other nuanced and more complex meanings of the term. Our driver was clearly just speaking his mind, perhaps unconsciously repeating what he had heard others say. After all, Boko Haram founder Mohammed Yusuf used to preach openly at mosques and in squares, traveling widely from his base in Maiduguri to neighboring states like Bauchi, Gombe, Yobe, and Kano. Cassette tapes of his sermons were—and perhaps still are—widely available on the streets and at mosques. Videos of his lectures and debates are available on YouTube.

My hotel, the Satus, was a rather popular destination, especially for foreign NGO workers, and it was easy to see why.

Located off a busy, gridlocked street (locals told me there had been construction work on this five-mile stretch of road for over five years), it was only a few minutes from all the central parts of Maiduguri. The hotel was hidden behind huge walls, like most buildings in the area. Neighbors usually merged their compounds together, creating large private neighborhoods inside tall dividers.

The hotel swimming pool was deserted. It was hard to imagine anyone packing swimming trunks and bikinis as they prepared to come to Maiduguri. Sharia law had not been kind to the hospitality industry; hotels and restaurants were viewed with suspicion and distrust. The receptionist, a young man named Daniel from the southern part of the country, told me the hotel generators were turned on at 5:00 p.m. daily. The National Electric Power Authority was legendary for its unreliability. The rooms were reasonably clean, and the service was tolerably efficient. I was lucky to get a room without prior reservation, he told me. They usually had a long waiting list of mostly NGO workers.

I met a few of them in the restaurant. Some had the look of long-term residents; they all had a wary, cautious air about them. Maiduguri was a town disoriented by the insurgency, and though it was slowly returning to normal, you could tell from their body language the people had almost forgotten what normalcy was like, and it would take a while for them to regain their balance. This had been, and still was, a veritable war zone.

76 Bombs had exploded in hotels and in mosques and churches, preachers had been slaughtered in front of their congregations and in their homes, sons had killed their fathers and informed on their teachers, and neighbors had turned against neighbors. Every night curfew began at 9:00. It used to be as early as 6:00 p.m. during the state of emergency in 2013. Almost every single person in the state had personal stories of close encounters with death at the hands of the military or Boko Haram. Even a child could point to a spot on the street where he or she had seen a dead body.

And that's exactly what Abbas, who had lived in Maiduguri all his life, did as he drove me around to point out important landmarks in the Boko Haram war. There, he said, pointing at one house front, was where a famous preacher, Mallam Ismail, was gunned down. The preacher had spoken out strongly against Boko Haram in his sermons. One day two young boys with Kalashnikovs followed his car, stopped him just off the main road, and told him they had come "to do God's work" before shooting him. Later Abbas pointed at some neem trees in which Boko Haram fighters hid overnight and came down in the morning and attacked the barracks. We passed the University of Maiduguri, where Abbas, who's twenty-seven, had graduated. But like most Nigerian graduates he had not secured employment, and was planning to go back for a master's degree. The University Teaching Hospital was where, during the 2009 Boko Haram uprising, there were

so many bodies in the streets they had to be brought by dump-
ster trucks to the mortuary, which overflowed and the dead
were piled up in the yard. The decomposing bodies smelled
so bad that people in the neighborhood deserted their homes.
The Gwange burial ground is the main cemetery for Muslims. It is surrounded by shoulder-high walls with an ungated
entrance through which a constant stream of people passed on
their way to burials. This was where early Boko Haram members were attacked by soldiers during that first blow in what
would turn out to be the bloodiest conflict Nigeria had seen
since the Biafran War in 1967.

The incident took place on June 11, 2009, when the sect followers were on their way here to bury some members who had
died in a car crash. Most of them were riding motorbikes, and
they were stopped by soldiers for not wearing helmets. The
helmet law had just been introduced in the country, and in
most places it had met with noisy opposition and demonstra-
tions, especially by bike operators who saw the law as nothing
but another opportunity for the police to extort money from
them. It was not exactly clear why the Boko Haram members
decided not to wear helmets, but their aversion toward anything
to do with the state and its laws was well established. They were
harassed and some say shot at by soldiers belonging to the Operation Flush II, and seventeen of them were taken to the hospital.

The clash was the culmination of an ongoing conflict
between the state government and the sect, which had recently

78   grown bolder in its condemnation of Ali Modu Sheriff, the
governor. Sharia law had been declared in the state, but Boko
Haram founder Mohammed Yusuf wanted an even stricter version in place, where schools would be segregated between boys
and girls, adulterers would be stoned, and thieves would be
amputated—the full works. Sheriff had promised Yusuf that it
would be done, so Boko Haram worked to ensure the governor
was returned to office. But after winning reelection Sheriff
reneged on his promise. The enraged Yusuf began to openly call
the governor an infidel. The incident at Gwange appeared to
be a ploy by the government to goad the sect into an open con-
frontation so as to have the opportunity to outlaw and suppress
it. After Gwange, Yusuf declared war on the government. In a
lecture titled "An Open Letter to the Government," he ranted,

> Why do they not attack other citizens, only us who believe
> in Allah and His Prophet? Whose property have we ever
> destroyed? Who is it we slaughtered like a ram? Who is it
> did we enter their houses and ransacked them? Just because
> we said Allah said, and the Prophet said, then they detest us
> because of our turbans—And yet this is not enough, they have
> to shoot us with their guns. This is my explanation. We will
> no longer listen to anyone. Their time is up. We will no longer
> accept invitations for mediation from anyone. We will not
> accept the shooting of twenty of our members, and we will not
> let it go, and we will not listen to anyone anymore.

Here we have the beginning of the narrative of victimhood and persecution that Boko Haram would adopt. In those early days the group was scrupulous in explaining its motives after every attack. It even had a Chief Information Officer, Abu Qaqa, who sent out emails and gave interviews to claim credit for attacks, or to correct perceived false representations of the group.

The response to Yusuf's declaration of war was immediate. In Maiduguri, two sect members, Hassan Sani Balami and Isa Viga Gwoza, decided to make a bomb and blow up public buildings. In Bauchi, Boko Haram members attacked a police station and tried unsuccessfully to break into the armory to take weapons. Before the week was out the uprising would spread to parts of Yobe and Kano states, where police stations, government buildings, and prisons were attacked.

As the fighting escalated, military reinforcements were sent to Maiduguri. Tanks rolled into Markaz Ibn Taymiyyah, the mosque where Boko Haram members had barricaded themselves. Yusuf somehow escaped, but he was eventually discovered in his father-in-law's house, hiding in the goat pen. Videos of his interrogation, still available on YouTube, show him surrounded by policemen, looking calm and alert and confidently defending himself. Hours later he would be

80   dead—killed as he tried to escape, according to the govern-
      ment. There are pictures that show his bullet-riddled body,
      still in handcuffs.

          "Before he was killed, you should have been here on a
      Friday," a former follower of Yusuf said. "You would think a
      big party was going on here. The whole area would be lined
      by exotic cars as very powerful individuals went to see Yusuf.
      They went in cars with tinted glasses so nobody would be able
      to see them. That is why many people believed that the man
      was being sponsored by some very powerful individuals." But
      today, driving down a bumpy, dusty road toward Markaz Ibn
      Taymiyyah, it was hard to imagine the pomp and glory. The
      only imposing building in the neighborhood was the cav-
      ernous Nigerian Railway Terminal, abandoned years ago when
      the trains stopped running all over Nigeria. Thanks to poor
      management and neglect, the Nigerian Railway Corporation
      had entered a long period of decline following the country's
      independence, and it declared bankruptcy in 1988.

          Until recently, Boko Haram had occupied the residen-
      tial quarters that were originally built for railway workers, but
      were now riddled with bullet holes. They also slept in aban-
      doned train cars and used them to store arms. A pile of rubble
      amid a few upright pillars marked the site where the mosque
      once stood.

          Here Yusuf had presided over a vibrant community of
      his adherents. He was spiritual leader as well as judge and

benefactor to his followers. He settled disputes and arranged marriages. There were *madrassas* ran on strict Islamic code, and even a welfare system that provided microfinance and healthcare to its members. It was, as the cliché goes, a government within a government. Yusuf's stated aim was to create a parallel government run on strict sharia law, free of what he considered the corrupting influence of democracy, Western education, and Western ways of life.

Yusuf's ideology did not develop in a void, and in fact he was heavily influenced by a predecessor group commonly known as the Nigerian Taliban, which was formed when about 200 young students, some of them sons of prominent government officials, withdrew from Maiduguri and moved to Kannama, a small desert town in Yobe State, near the border with Niger. They got their name because of their professed admiration for the Taliban in Afghanistan and Pakistan, and they even dressed like them, in calf-length trousers, waistcoats, and beard. They called their desert camp Afghanistan.

They lived in Kannama for one year without incident, observing their strict version of Islam, a puritanical Salafism that accepted only the full implementation of sharia. But by 2003 a rift occurred between them and their host community over fishing rights, and this might have led to the authorities, who had been observing them, giving them notice to quit the area. Few had heard of them until on New Year's Eve, when they attacked a police station in Kannama. They also went to

82   the neighboring city of Damaturu to carry out further attacks.
      They were repelled; some were killed, others arrested.

         It is the stump of this dispersed group that later returned
      to Maiduguri to form the vanguard of the Yusuf sect that
      became Boko Haram. Many external factors may have played
      their part in the radicalization of the Kannama group, and the
      list includes America's global war on terror after September
      11; the Israeli occupation of Palestine; the Iraq War; the U.S.
      invasion of Afghanistan. But local factors bore a weightier
      influence on the rise of radicalism in northern Nigeria.

         Apart from disgust with corruption and disaffection
      with the political system, the Kannama group was also dis-
      enchanted with Muslim leaders' tolerance of the status quo.
      They wanted change, not only in politics, but in religion as
      well. Their first target was the Sufi brotherhoods that had
      dominated religious life in the north for decades. Ever since
      the 1960s and '70s the Sālafi preacher Abubakar Gumi and
      the influential Izala Society had been lashing out against the
      Sufi brotherhoods. But Izala did not advocate violence against
      the state, instead seeking to take it over from within. (Boko
      Haram dismisses the Izala Society as infidels.) Gumi himself
      served as adviser on President Ibrahim Babangida's Council
      for Religious Affairs.

         To the Kannama group, there was no coexistence between
      state and religion. The state and its institutions were
      Western—specifically, British—inventions, and whatever

came from the West must have Judeo-Christian provenance,   83
and so must be rejected in favor of sharia. True Islamic reform
would require an overturning and overhauling of all institu-
tions of British-inspired government.

Yusuf surely lifted this anti-colonial fanaticism from
the Nigerian Taliban, but no one has been able to satisfacto-
rily place him at Kannama during the uprisings in 2003. There
have been various accounts of Yusuf's origins, with some
saying he began as an *almajiri*, begging on the streets for food.
Others say he went to university and even graduate school, but
later grew disillusioned with the system and turned against it.

What is clear is that Yusuf had been a rising star of the
Izala Society in Maiduguri's Indimi Mosque, where he was a
student under the famous preacher Jaafar Adam and became
the leader of the movement's youth wing, the Shababul Islam.
Most of the Nigerian Taliban started out in the Shababul Islam,
when the youths grew disenchanted with the Izala leadership
and decided to move to Kannama. Some say that Yusuf was
in Mecca performing the Hajj at the time, and Borno State's
deputy governor, Adamu Dibal, had to broker his return to
Nigeria. After meeting him several times, the deputy governor
called him brilliant. "He had this kind of monopoly in con-
vincing the youth about the Holy Koran and Islam," he said.

Because of his increasingly radical views Yusuf and his
followers were expelled from Indimi Mosque, and some say he
even had a hand in killing his Izala mentor, Jaafar Adam. He

84   moved his base and eventually built his Markaz Ibn Taymiyyah Mosque, on a plot of land on the Nigerian Railway Corpo-
ration quarters, given to him by his father-in-law. Eventually
his good fortunes ran out, and on July 11, 2009, he was killed
by the security forces.

The sector commander, a major in the army, was taking me
round some of the internally displaced persons camps around
Maiduguri to show me people recently rescued from Boko
Haram's increasingly shrinking "caliphate". The major was a
veteran of countless battles against Boko Haram, including one
in 2015 at Chibok. I had heard that Boko Haram had placed a 60
million naira bounty on his head, and when I asked the major
whether it was true, he laughed and said it was only 50 million.

    The first camp we went to was in a primary school, where
half of the classrooms had been transformed into living quarters for the refugees, while the other half were still used for les-
sons. So the refugees went about their daily business under the
full gaze of the students. The major told me that recently two
women in this camp had been asking to be released back to their
Boko Haram husbands in the forest. One was caught trying to
escape. I was shocked that they'd want to go back, but the major
said it was a common occurrence. Some were spies for Boko
Haram, posing as refugees, while with others it was a case of
Stockholm syndrome—they empathized so much with their
kidnappers and their cause that they wanted to go back to them.

The next camp was called the 500 Housing Estate, because the estate contained 500 housing units. The walls were unplastered and unpainted concrete, giving them a bombed-out feel. Some of the units had doors but no windows.

We saw mostly women walking about, children in tow. Most of the children did not belong to the women; they were orphans, abducted from their homes by Boko Haram or found wandering after the terrorists had killed their parents. For them the future held little promise, the boys would end up begging on the streets and the girls would most likely become prostitutes. It wasn't any easier for the women. Those who had spent time as Boko Haram "wives" also suffered from social stigma. They couldn't go back to their families, the perception being that they and the children they were forced to bear through rape were still brainwashed, and likely to become terrorists in the future.

Next to the 500 concrete houses were yet more rows of white plastic tents. There were more women, some cooking over open fire, others washing clothes and hanging them on lines. It was virtually a whole town of displaced persons.

"Who feeds them?" I asked the major.

"That is my biggest headache at the moment. The government is supposed to feed them, but it doesn't always work out. A few days ago some NGO workers came and gave them some food, rice, sugar. We haven't heard from anyone since then."

"Can't they go out to work?"

86   "We can't allow them, it is not safe."

Sourcing food for displaced persons wasn't part of his job description as sector commander, but the government couldn't always be relied upon. Abbas had told me of a camp next to his house where the refugees were completely abandoned, and the street behind the camp was soon covered with their trash and excrement, flung over the wall in plastic bags. Then, suddenly (just before a senatorial election), the government remembered them, and workers went to the camp and installed toilets and distributed food.

On the streets of Maiduguri it was normal to see long lines of women waiting in front of relief agencies for whatever they could get from the NGOs. Not all of them were refugees. Some were housewives impoverished by the war. The men—those not taken away and conscripted—had been killed, maimed, or simply rendered unproductive. The closing of the borders with Cameroon, Chad, and Niger had brought to a halt a flourishing international trade, which used to pass through Maiduguri and boost employment in the Chad Basin area.

The bulk of the refugees came from the villages, where the fighting had pushed Boko Haram. The irony was that some of these same people used to live in the cities, but they had run away to the villages—which were safer when Boko Haram was mainly an urban threat. They had sold their houses cheaply to get away. Now that Boko Haram had sacked and razed their houses in the villages, the camp was their only home.

There were hundreds of such camps all over the northeast, Yola, Bauchi, Gombe, Damaturu, Kano, and of course Maiduguri. And now that the war had spread into neighboring countries, there were camps in Chad, Niger, and Cameroon. There were camps run by churches and foreign organizations and individuals. There were camps for men, and camps for women. Recently, a camp had been started to rehabilitate repentant Boko Haram fighters. The program, "Operation Safe Corridor," would offer the ex-militants jobs and training in return for undergoing biometric profiling. About 800 fighters had already signed up, and there were plans to open more camps all over the northeast.

In most camps the conditions were appalling and ripe for the outbreak of diseases, and as if that wasn't bad enough, there were constant threats from Boko Haram infiltrators. Two days after I left Maiduguri, a bomb exploded in one of the camps, killing twenty-four people. A week later, two female suicide bombers killed at least fifty-eight in a camp in Dikwa, some fifty-five miles from Maiduguri.

The major said the attacks were aimed at discouraging displaced people from going to the camps, and forcing them to return to their towns and villages under Boko Haram rule, because the government couldn't protect them. "Their homes are not safe yet."

Return to Chibok

Part Three

Waiting for the Girls

The Maiduguri–Damboa road had been open for over a month now, since February 2016. We were gathered on the outskirts of Maiduguri in a convoy of over 200 cars, trucks, and buses. The road was still not 100 percent safe; it was right on the fringe of the Sambisa Forest where Boko Haram was making its last stand, and so cars could only travel with heavy military escort. Damboa, the last major town before Sambisa Forest, had been liberated since mid-2015, but only now had the road connecting it to Maiduguri been cleared of mines and declared safe for travel.

At exactly 9:00 a.m., the convoy set off, with military trucks in front and at the back, all mounted with machine guns, and outriders on motorbikes on the sides. There was nothing to see on either side of the road but dry grass and trees, mostly thorn trees clustered closely together. The roadside villages had been abandoned for up to four years now. In one village

92   piles of firewood by the roadside were still arranged exactly
the way the owners had left them when they escaped years
ago, except they were rotting. All the houses were gutted with
bullet holes, some the size of a fist. There were large bodies
of standing water, rather a surprise to see this late in the dry
season, but no villagers to use the water for their cattle. Fat
guinea fowls flew out of the bushes, unworried about hunters
or passersby.

Scattered by the sides of the road were black, cylindrical
objects that I at first mistook for chips of wood, or stones.
They were shell casings, which lined the sides of the road like
giant bird droppings all the way to Damboa. There were military camps at intervals, holding the space retaken from the
terrorists. We drove fast and quiet, swerving suddenly to
avoid giant craters in the road made by exploded IEDs. Soon
we were in Damboa. This was one of the towns hardest hit by
Boko Haram, and you could see evidence of it everywhere. By
the side of the road a church stood, the roof burned down, the
huge front door blackened by smoke.

I figured that by noon we should be in Chibok. The last time
I came the girls who were fortunate enough to escape initially
had been away at school, but now they were home for the Easter
break, and Ruth, who had arranged some interviews for my last
trip, said some of them were willing to meet me this time.

Our young driver was practically flying; the car slid in the
sand and dove into potholes. We were about fifteen minutes

outside Chibok when we came upon an accident. One of the
overloaded buses in the convoy lay in the middle of the road,
its wheels in the air. A man, his t-shirt soaked with blood,
waved at us and shouted, "Help, please help." Another man was
covered in blood from a deep cut on his head. Three others lay
by the side of the road, all covered in blood.

"I know these people," our driver said. "They are my neighbors in Maiduguri." We took our bags out of our car, folded
down the seats, and stretched out three of the bleeding men on
the floor. They were driven to the hospital, and Abbas and I got
a lift in another car.

Chibok market was as I remembered from two months
ago. Even some of the faces were recognizable: there was the
woman who charged people's phones from her generator
for twenty naira per charge; there was the woman who sold
water and soda and bread lying on a bench in front of her
shop; there was the same white, dusty pickup truck carrying
vigilantes on their way to a patrol; and there were the same
soldiers, with guns and without guns, coming out of shops
and going into shops. All looked the same—except the grain
seller's stand. Two days after my last visit, three suicide
bombers, dressed as women and riding bicycles, had stopped
at the town's checkpoint, where one of them exploded his
bomb, allowing the other two to enter town and attack the
market, killing thirteen people and destroying the grain
stand.

94   It was a depressing place, and the sadness was palpable in the hot, motionless air. Of course most of the sadness came from one's automatic association of Chibok with the kidnapped girls—it was like going to Hamelin and feeling the weight of the absent boys taken by the Pied Piper. We waited in Ruth's living room for our driver to return from the hospital so he could go and get the girls from their village, Mife. But one of the men had died on the way, and the driver had to stay back to give a statement, especially since he knew the man's family. In a strange twist of fate, it turned out these same men had wanted to hire our driver and his car for this trip, but they had contacted him late, so they had taken the bus. That night, another of the men would die as they waited to be attended to. So John, Abbas's friend, had gone to Mife on a bicycle to pick up the girls.

Ruth, who had been heavily pregnant the last time I was here, had given birth. This at least is good news, I thought. The baby had been sleeping, now he was awake; I watched her try to calm him down; when he quieted down she handed him to me. He was covered in a pink shawl—here people don't share Americans' obsession with color appropriateness for the genders.

I asked Ruth about Yana Galang, the parent who had shared her missing daughter's story the last time I was here. She was fine, Ruth said, but some of the parents were not. Since the kidnapping in 2014, at least eighteen parents had

died of stress-related illnesses like heart failure, stomach
ulcers, and hypertension. Boko Haram had killed a few others
in random attacks.

One day a depressed father had come to her house and
told her he simply couldn't continue to live knowing his
daughter was a Boko Haram prisoner in the forest, and soon
after his heart gave out and he died. Another father had dis-
appeared and couldn't be found for days. He was discovered wandering in the hills, shouting his daughter's name.
He said he was sure she was out there and could hear him.
He had lost his mind. Ruth said if you saw some of the parents walking in the village, it was as if there was no blood in
their bodies.

Many parents had carried out funeral rites for their
daughters and asked the government to declare them dead so
they could get a sense of closure. There were too many claims
of sightings, failed negotiations, and false rescues. One week,
two teenage girls, strapped with suicide vests and minutes
away from detonating them, had been apprehended by the
police in the village of Limani, a three-hour drive across the
border in Cameroon. One of them, a fifteen-year-old, claimed
to be a Chibok girl, but a few days later she was confirmed to
be from a different batch of Boko Haram abductees. The most
embarrassing miscue happened a day after the kidnapping,
when the Nigerian military's top spokesman claimed that "all
129 girls" except eight had been rescued, only to retract the

96   statement a day later, still unsure about the exact number of girls kidnapped.

A month after the kidnapping, and responding to increasing international and local pressures, President Goodluck Jonathan promised to visit Chibok and meet the parents of the missing girls. The next day he canceled the visit, saying it wasn't necessary, because it wouldn't bring back the girls. Only months later and at the urging of Pakistani Nobel Peace Prize laureate Malala Yousafzai, who visited Nigeria on her seventeenth birthday, did Jonathan meet the parents.

The government, it was later revealed, wasn't convinced that a kidnapping had taken place. In April 2014 the government was busy preparing to host the World Economic Forum in May. Political and world leaders were expected. The Jonathan government wanted to showcase Nigeria as an economic success story, and suspected that political opponents concocted the kidnapping story to sabotage the event. Even after the authorities confirmed the kidnapping, the administration did its best to downplay the seriousness of the event.

The Bring Back Our Girls campaign put the severity of the kidnapping beyond any doubt, as celebrities and politicians, including First Lady Michelle Obama, put pressure on the government to act and #BringBackOurGirls. Government officials were so frustrated that the finance minister, Okonjo-Iweala, was shown on TV telling an ABC News reporter, "I am tired of talking about the same thing!"

Most Nigerians were beginning to despair of the Jonathan government's cluelessness and lack of empathy. To them this was a further proof of the increasing disconnect between the administration and the concerns of the masses. Goodluck Jonathan never took the Boko Haram fight seriously, and considered it a northern problem, fomented by northern politicians to make the country "ungovernable" for a southerner like him. When he saw that his government was going to lose the elections in February 2015, he suddenly postponed them, saying he needed time to fight Boko Haram in the northeast so the people there could vote. Elections were rescheduled for May, and he lost anyway. For the first time in Nigerian history an incumbent party lost to a challenger, and many believe the bad handling of the fight against Boko Haram was a major reason why.

Evidence of mass corruption that went on under the Jonathan government in the name of the fight against terror is now beginning to emerge. National Security Advisor Sambo Dasuki is currently on trial for allegedly misappropriating billions of dollars budgeted for purchasing weapons and helicopters for the fight against terror. The money was reportedly funneled to party officials for Jonathan's reelection bid in 2015. When soldiers complained about the lack of equipment for the fight, Dasuki called them cowards.

In 2014, seventy-seven soldiers were court-martialed for mutiny, some of them having refused to go to the frontlines, saying they had not been paid their salaries or lacked proper equipment. Sixty-six of them were sentenced to death, but the new Buhari government has commuted the death sentences.

Former defense chief Alex Sabundu Badeh has also been arrested and accused of having skimmed over $1.5 million every month from his men's salary for years. Corruption may have even scuttled ransom negotiations for the girls. A top Jonathan aide, Hassan Tukur, had boasted of enlisting the help of Chadian President Idriss Déby in negotiating for the release of the Chibok girls. The office of the National Security Advisor gave Tukur $40 million for the negotiation, but Turkur allegedly gave Déby only $5 million, and kept the rest himself. He was arrested and granted bail of $40 million. He paid it.

The increasingly desperate Goodluck Jonathan even allowed a retired Australian clergyman to negotiate with Boko Haram. Stephen Davis had a record of dealing with Nigerian militants, and he was part of a 2014 ceasefire struck between the government and the militant Movement for the Emancipation of the Niger Delta, or MEND. The Chibok girls were likely being held by different groups at a number of locations, some in Cameroon. Davis claimed to have made contact with a Boko Haram faction there, and that they were willing to release eighteen—later reportedly raised to sixty—of the kidnapped girls in exchange for compensation for widows of slain

Boko Haram fighters and job opportunities for their members
if they surrendered. There was supposedly an appointed location for the hand-off, but Davis said he arrived hours late and
by then no one was there.

America

Before my trip to Maiduguri and Chibok, I had stopped in Jos to talk to Becky and Paul Gadzama, owners of the Education Must Continue Initiative, an NGO focused on working with Boko Haram victims. They ran schools in refugee camps in Yola, and their house in Jos was full of children rendered homeless by the war. Their humanitarian zeal was driven by their Christian belief, and also by their personal experience of Boko Haram. The Gadzamas were from Lassa, which had been overrun by Boko Haram. Two of their nieces had been kidnapped by Boko Haram, and their family house was burned down by the terrorists. "Their aim," Becky said, "is to stop education, especially that of young girls." That was why they named their NGO the Education Must Continue Initiative.

Becky had been in Lassa the day of the Chibok kidnapping; she had gone there to give a talk on education, something she did regularly for her NGO. She only heard about the

kidnapping the next day, and at the time she never knew she
was going to get involved with the girls. But that week she got
a call from Emmanuel Ogebe, a Nigerian human rights lawyer
based in Washington, D.C., who said that U.S. Rep. Christo-
pher H. Smith, a Republican from New Jersey, was in Nigeria
and would like to meet and hear the testimony of those who
escaped. Could she arrange to bring one of the girls to Abuja?

The Gadzamas arranged a meeting between Smith and a
girl and her father.

Five more members of Congress came to Abuja wanting
to speak to more of the girls, particularly those who had been
to the terrorists' stronghold in Sambisa before escaping. The
Gadzamas sent for more girls, assuring the parents that they
were in safe hands and no harm would come to them.

The Gadzamas noticed that many of the girls were in bad
shape. One of them had fractured her leg when she jumped off
the truck in her escape, and she needed better medical atten-
tion. Another was not being properly taken care of and had
developed a bad cough. That's when the Gadzamas decided to
send some of them to the U.S. The girls moved to the Gadzamas house in Jos and stayed there for a few months while
their visas were being processed. To protect the girls the Gadzamas told no one about the plan, not even their pastor, until
the day before they were to leave Nigeria.

They were sent to Ogebe, who took them into his home
in Virginia. Secrecy, silence, all in a bid to protect the girls,

was a theme I kept coming across. In America, where the girls had been giving testimonies to newspapers and even before the U.S. Congress, they always wore dark glasses to hide their identity, presumably from Boko Haram sympathizers who might be tempted to harm them.

As it turns out, I live only a few miles away from Ogebe, and we arranged to meet. Ogebe's humanitarian work involved advocacy for Christians in the predominantly Muslim northern Nigeria, where he believes there's a systematic plan to rid the region of all Christians. He was a prolific contributor of op-eds, had appeared on CNN and BBC to champion his cause, and was invited to give testimonies before the U.S. House Foreign Affairs Subcommitee on Africa, Global Health, Global Human Rights, and International Organizations. In one of his presentations he accused the U.S. of inadvertently aiding Boko Haram by not selling arms to the Nigerian government. Before receiving the Chibok girls he had already taken in two daughters of Christian clergymen killed by Boko Haram.

I asked how the girls were doing. They were well, he said, and one of them had finished high school and would soon be going on to college. For the rest of them, however, school remained a big challenge. When they first arrived their level of education was found to be far below that of their American age cohort. Even though back home they had been about to graduate secondary school, most of them had to start again

from middle school in America. His biggest concern now was
raising money for their college education. He had made over-
tures to the Nigerian embassy, but they had been keeping him
at arm's length. "To be honest I don't think they like us very
much," he said. "I think they are trying to shut us down."

Indeed, two weeks later the Nigerian government took
over guardianship of the girls from him. Ogebe was not pre-
viously notified, and found out about it through a terse
announcement in the newspapers, which claims that the parents of the girls had signed over their daughters to the Nigerian government, thus voiding any previous arrangements. It
was like "a military takeover of the girls by decree," he said.

A few days before I met Ogebe, he had been elated by the
first and so far only actual good news about the Chibok girls
since the abduction two years ago. JTF vigilantes had found
Amina Ali Nkeki near the Sambisa Forest, in a village where
she was hiding from Boko Haram. With her was her four-
month-old baby and a man who claimed to be her husband—a
captive, she said, forced to be a fighter, who was ordered by
Boko Haram to marry Nkeki before escaping with her. Nkeki is
the only one of the 219 girls to be rescued to date.

Ogebe told me that a year earlier, Boko Haram had once
again attacked Chibok. One of the women in the group, who
was with two men at the time, ran across an old woman.

"I am Amina," the girl told the old woman in the local
language, one that the two men did not understand. "My

104   mother's name is Binta in the village of Mbalala. Please tell her you saw me."

"Amina Ali, the one who got away, was not only exceptionally lucky," Ogebe wrote me in an email. "She had been trying to get out for a long time."

The Day They Took Us

Nkeki's rescue was still over a month away the day I waited for the Chibok girls in Ruth's living room.

At last, three of them arrived, dressed in their best wrappers, blouses, and head-ties. They leaned their bicycles against the wall and entered the house, one after the other. I watched them kneel to greet Ruth, speaking in the Kibaku language, and then they sat on the floor. It was good to see them face-to-face finally.

"So," I said in Hausa, "you are the Chibok girls."

The girls, Hauwa, Ladi, and Juliana, looked at one another, confused. One mumbled something about not being from Chibok.

"But the world only knows you as the Chibok girls, the ones that escaped," I said.

Hauwa, Ladi, and Juliana were actually from the nearby village of Mife. They had started school in Chibok three years

before the kidnapping, and they all belonged to the same res-
idence hall. They had shared so much together, and were still
sharing. They sat in a companionable huddle. As they talked,
one would occasionally interrupt to add something or correct
a particular point. I was speaking Hausa, and whenever I asked
something complex, Ruth would step in to translate it into the
local language, Kibaku, in which the girls were more fluent. It
took a while, but gradually they relaxed.

That day they went to school together from Mife, all three
of them on the same motorbike. They arrived at around 8:00
in the morning and took their exams, which was on geography.
Afterward Ladi wanted to go home. "There was a wedding,"
Ladi remembered. "I knew the people getting married. But the
security at the gate said I couldn't go. The vice principal was
also there. No one was allowed to go out that day."

That night the girls were sleeping out in the yard because
of the heat when they heard the gunshots. Some said they
should run away, others said no. At first, when the Boko
Haram men came into their dorms, the girls had thought
they were part of the school security because of their military uniforms.

"There were soldiers usually guarding the school?"

"Yes, but not that many. About five or so."

"What did they do first when they came?"

"They took away our cell phones. Then they asked, 'where
are the boys?' But we told them the boys were day students."

"Then they told us to gather in one place. They said they were there to protect us from Boko Haram, who were attacking the town. Then some of them started saying, 'Allahu Akbar.' That was when we realized they were not soldiers. They were Boko Haram."

"What else did they do?"

"They asked us for the engine block [brick making machine]. We said there wasn't one, and they said they'd search, and if they found it they'd shoot us. Next they asked for the admin office. Then they marched us out of the hostel to the gate."

"Where did they say they were taking you?"

"Well, they said we were not students, we were just prostitutes. They called us kafirai [infidels] and said we ought to be married. They said they'd take us somewhere near Maiduguri and dump us there."

They had taken some foodstuff and pots and pans from the store, then set the school buildings on fire. They led the girls to a nearby village, Mboa, where cars and trucks were parked.

"They told us to get in."

They were in the very first truck to leave. There were Boko Haram members sitting with them. Juliana, who at 16 was the youngest of the girls, remembered some of the men were perhaps younger than her.

"Did they talk to you in the truck?"

"No, they kept calling us infidels, that's all."

"Did they talk amongst themselves?"

"They spoke Hausa to us, but to each other they were speaking in a strange language we didn't know."

"Kanuri," Ruth said.

On the way the men stopped and set on fire the foodstuff and the pots and pans they had taken from the school store.

"Why?"

"We don't know."

The girls began throwing their shoes and scarves off the truck, hoping to mark a trail that would lead a rescue party to wherever they were being taken, like Hansel and Gretel's white pebbles and bread crumbs. "One girl said we should jump," Ladi said. But that night the moon was shining bright, and there were Boko Haram on motorbikes right behind the truck. But as they drove farther the less choice they had, so they started jumping. Some girls were picked up by the bikers and dumped back into the truck.

"We jumped down and started running into the bush. We ran for hours."

"I held onto a tree and jumped," Ladi said. After landing on her feet she and three other girls ran all the way back to school in the morning. "Our parents were there. They took us home."

"What happened after the escape?"

"Nothing."

Of the fifty-seven girls who escaped, thirteen were Muslims and had been sent to a school in Katsina, and forty-one, including Hauwa, Ladi, and Juliana, were enrolled in a Christian secondary school in Jos. But ten of them had since dropped out.

"Do you enjoy school?"

They looked at each other. Then Ladi, who appeared to be the boldest, said, "It was tough in the beginning. We were all scared. I used to cry all the time. But it is better now."

"Do you get visitors? Like people from the government?"

"No, not really. The principal [from Chibok] came to see us once."

"And what do you want to become when you go to university?"

They all wanted to become doctors.

"What, none of you wants to be a teacher?" Ruth asked.

Her husband, who had been quiet, asked the girls, "Do you know my brother's daughter, Esther? She had no exam that Monday, until Tuesday, but she insisted on going back to school that day. She was taken. Do you know her?"

"Yes," the girls nodded eagerly. "Esther, short, fair. She was in C class with us. We were in the same class."

They mentioned a few more names of their classmates who had been taken.

"Do you miss them?"

They nodded silently.

There was really nothing new in their story. Except for the particular details, it was the same story I had read in the

110   papers, the same story told by the girls in America in their various interviews. They woke up to sounds of gunfire, they were
herded into trucks, and they jumped off and ran into the night.
There was nothing more to tell. Surely, their interviewers
must tell themselves, there had to be something more, some
individual act of valor, some unique observation? But there
wasn't. The shocking banality of it.

Hauwa, Ladi, and Juliana were ordinary girls, young
enough to be my daughters, who had been raised to almost
mythic status by their extraordinary experience. The same
could even be said about many Boko Haram members, who
were ordinary boys in dirty shirts and slippers, shooting at
whatever they were told to shoot at by their handlers. When
I was a child, I remember seeing a picture of Maitatsine after
he had been killed. I had almost expected to see a two-headed
monster, but he was just a middle-aged man with one bad
eye and an emaciated body. This ordinary man was capable of
extraordinary acts of evil, but Hauwa, Ladi, and Juliana were
ordinary girls who had taken a leap of faith off that truck and
into the night, and that had made the difference between them
and those who were taken. Like most things in life, it all came
down to chance, opportunity, and desperation. There was no
single explanation.

It was getting dark. We took some pictures. The girls shyly
struck poses. Then it was time to go. They said goodbye and
pushed their bikes to the exit, and they were gone.

Acknowledgments

I want to thank my friends and family in Abuja, Maiduguri, Chibok, and Gombe who helped with words of encouragement, suggestions, logistics, and with a place to stay while I was carrying out the research for this book. They are too many to mention, and some are already mentioned in this book, but I must add to this list Mike Jimoh, James Jawur, Tina Wakawa, my cousin Monica and her husband Dr. Saliba, Adamu Ismaila, Ibrahim ("Blow") Abdullahi, and my cousin Murtala Atomanson. I couldn't have written this book without your assistance.

FURTHER READING   117

Violence in Nigeria: The Crisis of Religious Politics (University of Rochester Press, 1998), by Toyin Falola, a history professor at the University of Texas at Austin, provides well-researched, accessible, and multi-disciplinary background to religious uprisings in Nigeria from independence to the turn of the century.

In his Brooking's Institution Analysis Paper, "'The disease is unbelief': Boko Haram's Political and Religious Worldview," Alex Thurston places Boko Haram in an international perspective, comparing it to similar terror groups around the world and assessing its potential threat to America. He also makes useful suggestions on ways to defeat the group. https://www.brookings.edu/research/the-disease-is-unbelief-boko-harams-religious-and-political-worldview/

For a succinct analysis of inter-religious tensions in Nigeria, read "Christian-Muslim Relations in Northern Nigeria since the Introduction of Shari'ah in 1999" by Frieder Ludwig in *Journal of the American Academy of Religion* (Vol. 76, No. 3, Sep. 2008).

"Boko Haram and the Kidnapping of the Chibok Schoolgirls" by Jacob Zenn in the CTC Sentinel (May 2014, Vol. 7, Issue 5) is very useful for understanding Boko Haram's operations and its link to international terror groups.

The implications and consequences of the preference for sharia law over secularism by Muslim groups in northern Nigeria is discussed and historicized in *Democratization and Islamic Law: The*

118   *Sharia Conflict in Nigeria* (Campus Verlag, 2008) by Johannes Har-
      nischfeger, a professor of German literature, ethnology, and polit-
      ical science.

      For an introductory reading on the emergence of Boko Haram and its
      operations in the northeastern region of Nigeria, and a background
      to intra-religious conflicts between Muslim groups, *Boko Haram:
      Islamism, Politics, Security and the State in Nigeria* (Tsehai Pub-
      lishers, 2015), a collection of essays by various Boko Haram scholars
      edited by Marc-Antoine Pérouse De Montclos, is invaluable.

      Andrew Walker, who was a BBC reporter based in Nigeria, had
      worked for the Nigerian publication Daily Trust for almost a
      decade. His *"Eat the Heart of the Infidel": The Harrowing of Nigeria
      and the Rise of Boko Haram* (Hurst, 2016) is a well-researched, acces-
      sible, and entertaining study of the history of Islam in northern
      Nigeria written from a reporter's perspective.

      Boko Haram: Nigeria's Islamist Insurgency (Hurst, 2015) by Virginia
      Comolli, a research fellow for security and development at the
      International Institute for Strategic Studies, provides a carefully
      detailed timeline of Boko Haram's emergence and terror attacks.

      Mike Smith, who was Agence France-Presse's bureau chief for part
      of West Africa from 2010 to 2013, presents a firsthand account of
      the rise of Boko Haram, especially its bombing of the UN building
      in Abuja, in his book, *Boko Haram: Inside Nigeria's Unholy War* (I.B.
      Tauris, 2015).

NOTES

19 emergency rule in 2013:
http://www.bloomberg.com/
news/articles/2013-05-14/
nigeria-s-jonathan-declares-
emergency-rule-in-3-northeast-
states

**20 Recently, Khalid Al-Barna-
wi:** http://www.bbc.com/news/
world-africa-35956301

**22 a "technical" victory over Boko
Haram:** http://www.bbc.com/
news/world-africa-35173618. See
also Lai Mohammed's efforts to
back up this claim: http://www.
premiumtimesng.com/news/
headlines/195668-we-have-
defeated-boko-haram-
december-deadline-met-
nigeria-says-2.html

23 In a move clearly: http://www
.bbc.com/news/world-
africa-35189041

23 cleric Mohammed Yusuf: For
accounts of the rise of Boko Haram
and its early activities, see essay
collection edited by Marc-
Antoine Pérouse De Montclos,
*Boko Haram: Islamism, Politics,
Security and the State in Nigeria*
(Tsehai Publishers, 2015)

**25 targeting the Nigeria
Police:** http://www.bbc.com/news/
world-africa-13805688

26 at the UN headquarters:
http://www.cbsnews.com/news/
nigeria-un-office-hit-by-massive-
bomb-18-dead/

27 it was now intent: http://
www.longwarjournal.org/
archives/2014/08/boko_harams_
new_cali.php

27 Shekau pledged: On August 2,
2016, ISIS announced in its magazine that it had replaced Shekau
with Abu Musab al-Barnawi. The
new leader accused Shekau of
unjustifiably killing Boko Haram
commanders and fellow Muslims.
Shekau released a statement the
next day declaring he was still in
charge. https://www.theguardian.
com/world/2016/aug/05/isis-
tries-to-impose-new-leader-on-
boko-haram-in-nigeria

28 in the town of Buni Yadi:
http://www.reuters.com/arti-
cle/us-nigeria-violence-idUS-
BREA1P10M20140226

30 Chibok is perhaps: http://
metropole.ng/index.php/
component/k2/item/1893-a-
short-history-of-chibok

**46 One local government
chairman:** http://dailypost.
ng/2012/04/02/boko-haram-
kills-lg-boss-loses-3-members/

52 Why, one of them questioned:
https://www.youtube.com/
watch?v=695WIiyt014

122   58 **A critique of the *almajiri* system:** Virginia Comolli gives a thoughtful analysis of the *almajiri* system in her *Boko Haram: Nigeria's Islamist Insurgency* (Hurst, 2015).

58 **That version of Islam:** "Boko Haram and Its Muslim Critics: Observations from Yobe State" by Johannes Harnischfeger in *Democratization and Islamic Law: The Sharia Conflict in Nigeria* (Campus Verlag, 2008).

59 **Marwa was originally from Cameroon:** Both Toyin Falola and Andrew Walker have lengthy sections on the Maitatsine uprisings in their books. Falola: *Violence in Nigeria: The Crisis of Religious Politics* (University of Rochester Press, 1998). Walker: *"Eat the Heart of the Infidel": The Harrowing of Nigeria and the Rise of Boko Haram* (Hurst, 2016).

66 **On Feb 14, 2015:** https://www.theguardian.com/world/2015/feb/14/boko-haram-launches-first-attack-in-chad

66 **Usman dan Fodio:** Andrew Walker is especially detailed in his analysis of the Usman dan Fodio jihad.

67 **"The area became a virtual slave farm":** Falola, *Violence in Nigeria*.

71 **"I took your girls":** Boko Haram propaganda video, May 5, 2014. https://www.youtube.com/watch?v=wrfWS_vLoD4

77 **The incident took place on June 11:** See Abdalla Uba Adamu's "Insurgency in Nigeria: The Northern Nigerian Experience"

78 **Yusuf declared war on the government:** Ibid.

80 **"Before he was killed, you should have been here on a Friday":** http://kayodeogundamisi.blogspot.com/2011/12/boko-haramhistoryideas-and-revolt-by.html

80 **presided over a vibrant community:** See Kyari Mohammed, "The Message and Methods of Boko Haram" in ed. Johannes Harnischfeger, *Democratization and Islamic Law: The Sharia Conflict in Nigeria*.

82 **Apart from disgust:** Ibid.

83 **Yusuf was in Mecca:** Mike Smith's *Boko Haram: Inside Nigeria's Unholy War* (I.B. Tauris, 2015) is especially authoritative on the rise of Yusuf and the Kannama events.

85 **Boko Haram "wives":** https://www.yahoo.com/news/fear-violence-kidnapping-life-women-under-boko-haram-004726933.html

87 **"Operation safe corridor":** There's a whole website that

documents the activities of the government on this: https://www.informationng.com/tag/operation-safe-corridor

87 **a bomb exploded in one of the camps:** http://www.aljazeera.com/news/2016/02/suicide-bombers-hit-nigerian-displaced-persons-camp-160210184351280.html

95 **One of them, a fifteen-year-old:** https://news.vice.com/article/child-suicide-bomber-in-cameroon-is-not-missing-chibok-girl

96 **at the urging of Pakistani:** http://www.bbc.com/news/world-africa-28292480

96 **"I am tired of talking about the same thing!":** http://abcnews.go.com/International/video/nigeria-official-tired-talking-kidnapped-girls-23660668

97 **Sambo Dasuki:** https://www.ft.com/content/fe389208-a718-11e5-9700-2b669a5aeb83

97 **soldiers were court-martialed:** http://www.premiumtimesng.com/news/headlines/195425-nigeri-an-military-commutes-death-penalty-of-66-soldiers-to-jail-terms.html

98 **A top Jonathan aide:** http://saharareporters.com/2016/05/21/president-jonathans-top-aide-hassan-tukur-detained-over-chibok-girls-40m-scam

98 **Stephen Davis had a record:** http://www.abc.net.au/news/2014-08-27/australian-risks-life-to-rescue-kidnapped-nigeri-an-girls/5699676

103 **Nigerian government took over:** http://www.premiumtimesng.com/news/more-news/204480-guardian-chibok-girls-u-s-lambasts-nigeria-taking-girls-decree.html

103 **Nkeki is the only one:** http://www.bbc.com/news/world-africa-36330379

Is This the Downfall of Boko Haram?

My last visit to Maiduguri and Chibok was over a year ago, on Easter Sunday. Since then a lot has happened, including the negotiated release of twenty-one Chibok schoolgirls in October 2016. Before then, one Chibok girl, Amina Ali Nkeki, was discovered wandering in Sambisa Forest with her child on May 17. Amina was the first to be released from captivity since the night more than two hundred schoolgirls were abducted by the terrorist group Boko Haram in 2014. Another girl, Maryam Ali Maiyanga, was discovered almost by accident on November 5 in an internally-displaced-person's camp by soldiers routinely screening escapees from Boko Haram's base in the Sambisa Forest. She was carrying a ten-month-old baby boy. According to her, the boy's father was a Boko Haram fighter and had been killed in battle. And in the first week of January 2017, the Nigeria military announced the rescue of another Chibok girl, Rakiya Abubabakar; she was also with a ten-month-old son.

That's twenty-four girls out of 218, a mere trickle. But could this trickle soon turn into a flood? Would we soon see the return of *all* the remaining Chibok schoolgirls? Everyone hopes so, but no one knows if it will ever happen. The administration of Nigerian President Muhammadu Buhari is holding its cards close to its chest.

126   Governments usually don't want to be seen to be negotiating with terrorists. The release of the twenty-one girls in October was made through a convoluted process that included the Swiss government and the Red Cross as go-betweens. Some reports say the girls were released in exchange for four imprisoned Boko Haram commanders and money amounting to millions of dollars. The Buhari administration has denied giving anything in exchange for the girls, though common sense would suggest Boko Haram would never release the girls for free. In August, Abubakar Shekau, the group's leader, released a video in which his spokesman, Abu Zinnira, indicated their willingness to swap the girls for imprisoned Boko Haram fighters. The video showed some of the Chibok girls in custody, stating that others had died in military bombardments (a claim later corroborated by Amina Ali Nkeki). Zinnira also listed certain trusted journalists and individuals the government could use as intermediaries if they wanted to negotiate with Boko Haram.

Why was Boko Haram suddenly keen to negotiate with the government? There have been attempts at deals in the past, but most of them have proved fruitless, as Boko Haram certainly recognizes the schoolgirls' practical worth as hostages and symbolic value as propaganda. The reason for this change of mind is most likely traceable to the rift in the ranks of the terror group. In 2015, Shekau had publicly declared allegiance to ISIS. In August 2016, in its propaganda magazine *al-Nabā*, ISIS announced that it had ousted Shekau as leader of Boko Haram and named as his replacement Abu Musab al-Barnawi, who is believed to be the son of Boko Haram's charismatic founder, the late Mohammed Yusuf. In a spat that played out in the media, al-Barnawi accused Shekau of being a psychopathic killer, and went on to list names of comrades Shekau had slaughtered for various flimsy reasons. He painted a picture of a demented Shekau, holed up in his stronghold, surrounded by luxuries and women, while al-Barnawi sent his fighters to die for him.

Another reason for the split is over doctrine. Whereas Shekau still believes in *takfir*—denouncing and killing non-Muslims as well as Muslims who disagree with his principles—al-Barnawi rejects the killing of Muslims and the bombing of mosques, preferring to focus his jihad on Christians and foreigners. After the split, al-Barnawi controlled most of the border regions in northern Borno, while Shekau and his faction controlled the central regions around Sambisa Forest.

Violent clashes between the two factions have been reported in remote villages near the border between Nigeria and Niger. This weakening of the terror group would seem to account for the recent successes the government troops are scoring against Boko Haram. In the dying days of 2016, videos were shown of the Nigerian troops setting ablaze "Camp Zero", said to be Boko Haram's final redoubt, deep in Sambisa Forest. A recovered jihadist flag was handed to the president Buhari by the military commanders. In a message to the troops, the president said, "The terrorists are on the run, and no longer have a place to hide. I urge you to maintain the tempo by pursuing them and bringing them to justice." One glaring fact though still remains— none of the remaining Chibok girls was discovered in Camp Zero, and neither was Abubakar Shekau captured or killed. Meaning, even though the momentum seems to be on the side of the government troops, the fight against Boko Haram is still far from over. Until all the remaining Chibok girls are returned, or at least accounted for — until the over 10,000 hostages said to be stuck in remote villages and towns still under threat from roving Boko Haram fighters are rescued — the war would not have been won. It took nearly a decade for Boko Haram to become the terrible force it is, and defeating it and all vestiges of its hateful ideology will take time. Meanwhile, the search for the Chibok girls must continue.

Helon Habila, January 2017